AROUND the WORLD with JUSTIN BIEBER

AROUND the WORLD with
JUSTIN BIEBER

True Stories From
Beliebers Everywhere

Sarah Oliver

JOHN BLAKE

Published by John Blake Publishing Ltd,
3 Bramber Court, 2 Bramber Road,
London W14 9PB, England

www.johnblakepublishing.co.uk

www.facebook.com/Johnblakepub facebook
twitter.com/johnblakepub twitter

This edition published in 2014

ISBN: 978 1 78219 898 7

British Library Cataloguing-in-Publication Data:

A catalogue record for this book is available from the British Library.

Design by www.envydesign.co.uk

Printed and bound in Great Britain by CPI Group (UK) Ltd

3 5 7 9 10 8 6 4 2

Papers used by John Blake Publishing are natural, recyclable products made
from wood grown in sustainable forests. The manufacturing processes
conform to the environmental regulations of the country of origin.

Every attempt has been made to contact the relevant copyright-holders,
but some were unobtainable. We would be grateful if the
appropriate people could contact us.

Dedicated with love to James,
Daniel and Christopher

Sarah Oliver is an author from Widnes in Cheshire. She was the author of *Justin Bieber A–Z*, which has been translated into five languages. She also wrote the double biography of Harry Styles and Niall Horan, the book *One Direction A–Z*, which was a *Sunday Times* Best Seller, and *Robert Pattinson A–Z*.

Why not follow Sarah – @SarahOliverAtoZ – on Twitter?

CONTENTS

INTRODUCTION

As you read this book, you'll hear stories of when fans met Justin, his family and his crew. You'll find out what Justin thinks of the different countries he visits and the Bieber Parades that fans do for him. Justin might have been to lots of different countries to perform his concerts, but there are still countries he can't wait to visit – he wants to visit every country where there are Beliebers, which is the name for every true Justin Bieber fan.

You'll also find out what Justin is really like from the fans that have met him at concerts, signings and the hotels where he stays when he's touring. Some fans camp out for days to get tickets to see Justin or enter hundreds of competitions for the opportunity to win Meet & Greet wristbands.

CHAPTER 1

JUSTIN'S FAMILY & CREW

Before you start reading the stories contained in this book, it's a good idea to familiarise yourself with the people who make up Justin's family and crew.

PATTIE MALLETTE

Pattie is Justin's mom and her Twitter name is @pattiemallette. She has over 2.5 million followers. Pattie was eighteen when Justin was born and they are very close. She is a Christian and brought Justin up in the Church – so he learned about God and Jesus from a very early age. She split up from Justin's dad Jeremy when Justin was still a baby.

When Justin was asked during an interview for *The Oprah Winfrey Show* what he loves most about his mom, he said: 'I love that she's just a really strong woman – she's been there since Day One and just wanted me to be the best person that I can possibly be. She doesn't care about the money, the fame; she just wants to be my mom.'

Pattie is so proud of Justin and often sends him lovely tweets. Here are some of her best tweets: 'Luv u justin ur the best son ever. I'm glad ur so well behaved ur such an angel.'

'Ok so my phone died before I could finish my tweets! Congrats baby boy! You deserve the best & to God be all the glory!! "Pray" was AMAZING!'

'I just saw a screening of the best movie ever! #neversaynever So proud! & no. Its NOT a concert movie. Its an inspiring life story thus far!'

JEREMY JACK BIEBER

Jeremy is Justin's dad and his Twitter name is @Lordbieber. He has two young children, Jazmyn and Jaxon, with whom Justin has a great relationship. Jeremy and Pattie have a deep respect for each other and they do socialise together when they are with Justin. Justin explained to *Seventeen* magazine in June 2010 what it was like, growing up, to have divorced parents. He revealed: 'My parents weren't the type to talk trash about each other. Some parents, when they split up, the mom will say, "Your dad's a jerk," but mine were never like that. So that definitely made it easier for me. I knew they loved me, and they split up because of them, not because of me.

'I have a great relationship with my dad. When I was younger, he taught me how to play some songs on the guitar, like "Knockin' On Heaven's Door" by Bob Dylan. He's the one who got me into classic rock and then turned me on to stuff like Guns N' Roses and Metallica. He taught me how to drive too. He's cool.'

DID YOU KNOW?

Jeremy now works as a carpenter and construction worker but years ago he used to be a professional wrestler.

BRUCE & DIANE DALE

Justin has a huge extended family and he tries to see them as much as he can. He is particularly close to his grandparents, Bruce and Diane Dale. He speaks fluent French because some members of his family are French-Canadian and don't speak English.

DID YOU KNOW?

Justin's great-grandfather was originally from Germany.

Family means the world to Justin and he will always put them first. He looks to them for guidance and advice. He told *Us* magazine: 'My grandparents Bruce and Diane Dale [are my relationship role models]. They love each other so much, after so many years!

'When I'm their age, I want to be as in love with my wife as my grandfather is with his.'

RYAN BUTLER & CHAZ SOMERS

Ryan and Chaz are Justin's best friends from home. Their Twitter names are @itsryanbutler and @chazilla94 (Chaz hasn't updated his Twitter account for a long time). Ryan is a writer and director now. To see some of his videos, go to http://vimeo.com/vkrb.

Justin, Ryan and Chaz have been the best of friends since they were seven or eight and started playing hockey together. They attended Stratford Central Secondary School and enjoyed messing around in class. When Justin got his record deal and moved to Atlanta in 2008, Ryan and Chaz were happy for their friend but sad at the same time because they would miss him loads. The three of them are still close now and Justin pays for Ryan and Chaz to fly out to see him whenever they can. He has other friends now but he will always be close to them because they knew him before he was famous and they shared some good times together.

Back in January 2010, Justin told journalist Nicholas Kohler from *Macleans.ca*: 'They [Ryan and Chaz] like me for me. When we're hanging out and I say something stupid or something, they're not going to treat me like I'm a superstar, by any means. They're not going to treat me like I'm bigger than everybody else. They're just going to treat me like Justin. They're going to pop me in the head and not care. I get to see them at least once a month. I get to fly them out to wherever I am. I've flown them out to L.A. and Atlanta. I think it's really important to just have your close friends around you. We're very active, we play basketball and hockey and soccer and stuff. We go to the movies with girls and stuff like regular teenage boys.'

CAITLIN BEADLES
Caitlin is a close friend and former girlfriend of Justin. Her Twitter name is @godsgirl8494.

When Justin was performing in Germany in August 2009, Caitlin nearly died in a boating incident.

Justin's friends left messages for him to tell him what had happened but Justin didn't get them until he returned home. As soon as he found out, he contacted Caitlin's family.

Justin explained to *Twist* magazine: 'I was scared, so I immediately called up Caitlin's family, and they weren't picking up the phone, so I got really nervous. I kept calling and texting, and finally I got in contact with Caitlin's mom. I talked to her on the phone for about 20 minutes and she was crying. It was tough. Caitlin's actually my ex-girlfriend, I dated her about six months ago, so it was hard because she's still a good friend.

'I went to the hospital to visit and she looked really bad. She had all of these IVs in her, and she couldn't speak at all. I brought her a Build-A-Bear because we had always wanted to make one together and we never got a chance to do it. So, I went and built her a bear and brought it to her in the hospital. I dressed it up as me; I even put a little baseball cap on it. Caitlin was very lucky that she survived, and now she's doing a lot better. She's in physical therapy where she's learning how to walk again, so that's good.'

Caitlin is much better now and meets up with Justin occasionally.

SCOOTER BRAUN

Scooter is Justin's manager but he is also like a big brother/father figure to him. His Twitter account is @scooterbraun.

Justin wouldn't be the star he is today without Scooter, as it was Scooter who discovered him. Scooter explained to *azcentral.com* how it happened: 'I was consulting for an act that Akon had in a production deal and looking at his YouTube videos. The kid was singing Aretha Franklin's "Respect," and there was a related video of Justin singing the same song. I clicked on it thinking it was the same kid and realized that the 20-year-old I was watching was now 12.'

As soon as Scooter had watched a few of Justin's other YouTube videos, he knew he had to track him down because he had so much talent. It took a while for Scooter to convince Justin's mom Pattie to allow him to manage her son but they haven't looked back since. He arranged for Justin to meet Usher and Justin Timberlake, who both wanted to sign him, and then, together, they decided that Usher would be the best mentor.

Scooter might be Justin's friend but when Justin oversteps the mark he isn't afraid to tell him off. He wants to protect Justin and won't let him be manipulated by people or do something he will regret later. Scooter told *YOU Magazine*: 'He is the son I didn't have. If he has done something wrong, he has to apologise. Justin isn't treated with kid gloves. I've sacked people who have pandered to him. He's a kid. He's not perfect. You have to set boundaries, consistencies.'

Justin wants to have a career as long as Michael Jackson's and Scooter is determined to help him achieve just that. Scooter revealed to *The Hollywood Reporter*: 'Justin doesn't study the people who made it, he studies the people who haven't. He hears all the naysayers about how he's going to disappear, so he likes to look up people who used to be the so-called Justin Biebers before him and didn't go anywhere. He wants to see why they didn't go anywhere. The general feeling we get is that it had nothing to do with their talent and everything to do with their personal life. Like the kids fall into drugs and destroy their own trajectory.'

KENNY HAMILTON

Kenny is Justin's bodyguard and his Twitter account is @kennyhamilton. Justin has known Kenny since the beginning of his career as he was a friend of Scooter's before he became a bodyguard. Kenny has nearly 2 million followers on Twitter.

Justin knows he can rely on Kenny to keep him

safe at all times. He is a close friend too, and Justin listens to what he tells him. If Kenny says he needs to get out of a location fast for his own safety, Justin does just that.

> **DID YOU KNOW?**
>
> Kenny thinks of Justin as his nephew.

RYAN GOOD

Ryan is Justin's swagger coach and stylist. His Twitter account is @thatrygood.

Justin explained to *Macleans.ca* what being his swagger coach involves: 'It's pretty simple, he kind of teaches me, he helps me just stay swaggerific. I don't know.'

The definition of 'swaggerific' is to have lots of confidence in the way you move and style.

When Justin does photo shoots for magazines and newspapers, usually he has no say in what he wears as an outfit will already have been picked out by a stylist from the publication. Most of the time Justin is quite open-minded but sometimes he has to refuse to wear an outfit, if it is truly awful. He told *Top of the Pops* magazine: 'Well, I try not to be rude, but people push and push you. I was at this photo shoot and these guys were like, "Put this on, it looks really cool," and I was like, "I don't really like that, I don't wanna wear that." This is me, I wear a hoodie, I'm just easy.'

USHER

Usher is Justin's mentor and close friend. His Twitter account is @usher. He sees Justin as his little brother, and when he first advised Justin he told him to 'stay humble, stay grounded, remember where you come from, family is really important and don't forget that', Justin revealed on *The Today Show*.

In April 2010, Usher told MTV: 'You haven't seen the best of him. He is a pop craze like The Beatles. They started out as pure pop artists and look what they became over the years.

'Justin reminds me of myself at that age, only he's a much more talented musician than I was. He taught himself piano and guitar. I couldn't, so he has that advantage.'

ALLISON KAYE

Allison is Justin's general manager on tour and PR. Her Twitter account is @allisonkaye. During Justin's Believe shows, she was the one who went out into the audience and picked out a Belieber to be the girl in the 'One Less Lonely Girl' performances.

CARIN MORRIS

Carin is Scooter's ex-girlfriend and her Twitter account is @CarinMB. Originally from Cape Town, South Africa, she is one of Justin's stylists.

JAN SMITH

Justin's vocal coach is Jan Smith (he calls her 'Mama Jan') and her Twitter account is @atlvox. She used to be Usher's vocal coach when he was a young singer.

Justin told *OK! Magazine* back in July 2010: 'Everyone's voice changes, puberty is a natural thing.

'I have the best vocal coach in the world and we're working on my voice and doing what I need to do. It's not like as soon as you hit puberty, you stop singing.'

Justin really admires Jan and is so grateful for everything she has done for him over the years. He had never had a vocal coach before because he couldn't afford singing lessons when he was growing up in Stratford, Ontario.

ALFREDO FLORES

Alfredo is a director and editor. He is one of Justin's best friends and Justin knows he can trust him. His Twitter account is @AlfredoFlores.

Alfredo told *Be Magazine*: 'Justin is like my little brother. As he gets older, he has become one of my best friends. At first, I was his big brother who talked to him about girls and tried to show him the way. Now that he is older, it's like we can talk about the same things and relate to each other in more ways than one. He is a great kid, with a great heart, and truly one of my best friends!'

JAMES 'SCRAPPY' STASSEN

Scrappy is Justin's stage manager and his Twitter account is @scrappy. In his Twitter bio, he says, 'Justin is a pleasure to work with… most of the time.'

JUSTIN ALAVI

Justin's drummer is called Justin Alavi and his Twitter account is @OtherJustin. He has over 18,000 followers and enjoys reading tweets Beliebers send him.

ROBERT CAPLIN

Robert is Justin's photographer and his Twitter account is @robertcaplin. He tours with Justin all around the world and takes as many photos as possible!

DAN KANTER

Dan is Justin's musical director and lead guitarist. He is also a talented songwriter and producer. His Twitter account is @dankanter. When Dan married

Yael Latner in October 2010, Justin, Dan and other members of Justin's crew performed 'Get Down Tonight' by KC and the Sunshine Band and the traditional Jewish song 'Hava Nagila'.

MUSICIANS

Tomi Martin and B Harv are Justin's guitarists. Their Twitter accounts are @Tomigunn and @IamBHarv. Justin's drummer is Melly and his Twitter account is @mellyinyourears. DJ James is Justin's DJ and his Twitter account is @DJTayJames. Justin's backup singers are Legaci (Micah Tolentino, Dominic Manuel, Delfin Lazaro, Chris Abad and Jason Atencion). The Twitter account for their group is @legacimusic.

DANCERS

Justin has lots of dancers who go on tour with him. These include: Marvin Millora (@MarvinMillora), Michael Vargas (@Michael_Vargas), Nick DeMoura (@NickDeMoura) and Anthony Carr (@AmountboyKanec).

CHAPTER 2

AMERICA

Justin might love America but he will never become an American citizen. He told *Rolling Stone Magazine*: 'Canada's the best country in the world. We go to the doctor and we don't need to worry about paying him, but here [America], your whole life, you're broke because of medical bills. My bodyguard's baby was premature, and now he has to pay for it. In Canada, if your baby's premature, he stays in the hospital as long as he needs to, and then you go home.'

When he's not touring, Justin lives in Calabasas, Los Angeles. He likes having his famous friends come over, and in August 2013 he tweeted: 'Chillin with the boys at home Kevin Durant, Tyson Chandler and Carl Lentz.'

Kevin and Tyson are professional basketball players and Carl Lentz is the pastor of Hillsong Church in New York. Justin has spent quite a bit of time with Carl and, in a message posted on Instagram a few months earlier, he wrote: 'Me and my homies @ryangood24 and @carllentz at lunch talking bout our saviour Jesus Christ.'

Justin has had so many memorable performances in America but one of the most special was performing at Madison Square Garden in August 2010. In his concert movie *Never Say Never* (2011), Justin says: 'There's gonna be times in your life when people tell you you can't do something. And there's gonna be times in your life when people tell you you can't live your dreams. And there's gonna be times in your life when people tell you you can't sell out Madison Square Garden! This is what I tell them: NEVER SAY NEVER!'

Selling out Madison Square Garden meant the world to Justin because it's such an iconic venue. The greatest singers of all time have performed there. When the tickets for Justin's show went on sale, they sold out in twenty-two minutes!

DID YOU KNOW?

During Justin's Madison Square Garden performance, he sang 'U Smile' and 'On Bended Knee' with Boyz II Men, 'Somebody to Love' with Usher, 'Overboard' with Miley Cyrus, 'Eenie Meenie' with Sean Kingston and 'Baby' with Ludacris.

Justin will never forget 22 December 2011 because this was the date he performed on *The X Factor 2011* final in Hollywood with the legendary Stevie Wonder. They sang 'The Christmas Song' together, and afterwards Justin tweeted: 'we went real BIG on X Factor 2nite. thank you to the legendary STEVIE WONDER and to @drewryniewicz who i hope realized dreams do come true.'

Drew was one of the *X Factor* contestants and she is a huge Belieber. In her first audition, she sang 'Baby' and during the show she performed 'Santa Claus Is Coming To Town' with Justin. She saw Justin's message that night and tweeted: '@justinbieber you rock! #NEVERSAYNEVER Performing with you was a dream,) thank youuuuuuuuuuu<3.'

Less than two weeks later, Justin had another huge performance to do, this time in Times Square, New

York. It was New Year's Eve and he was performing the Beatles' classic 'Let It Be'. He tweeted fans to say: 'u know what..to say thank you for an amazing 2011, me and @officialjaden are releasing a #NewYears song at Midnight. #COUNTDOWN.

'New Years is starting all around the world. so to all my fans around the world... THANK YOU FOR 2011 and Have a Great 2012. I LOVE U.'

DID YOU KNOW?

After midnight Justin and his crew held their own party, which went on until the early hours.

Another of Justin's American highlights was in May 2010, when he was interviewed by the chat-show legend Oprah Winfrey. It meant the world to him and to his whole family. The episode in which he featured was called 'World's Most Talented Kids'. Justin was asked what it was like to go from being a schoolboy to becoming a big star, and how he feels about fame and his fans. During the show, he surprised three sisters who had been due to see him in concert but, because their soldier dad had been deployed to Iraq, they couldn't go. Justin gave them front-row tickets to his concert and took them on a limo ride. Oprah arranged for their dad to appear on Skype from Iraq, and he said: 'Oprah, you just made me Father of the Year for the next decade.'

Justin told the girls' dad: 'When you get back, we're going to have five tickets waiting for you and your family to come to my concert on my tour.'

Once filming finished and Justin left the studio, he tweeted: 'Just got to say that Oprah is real nice down-to-earth person. She even came back after the show to talk with everyone. She is incredible. And she made my grandpa cry. He went all water works in the crowd.'

On his official Facebook page, he wrote: 'Couldn't believe she [Oprah] was interviewing me. It was surreal. Thanks to everyone who worked hard to get me there. Really an honor and a testament to the incredible fans that you all are. Thank you. Really.'

Pattie tweeted: 'So proud!!! My son just did Oprah! @justinbieber was so charming! It airs May 11th! I was on for a minute too!! So exciting!'

Justin has had the opportunity to perform in front of some very influential people, including the President of the United States, Barack Obama. The first time Justin met President Obama was on Sunday, 13 December 2009. Justin had been invited to take part in the *Christmas in Washington* Special with his good friend and mentor Usher. The charity show was broadcast on TV and the money raised went to the National Children's Medical Center, a cause chosen by the President's wife, Michelle Obama.

Before he took to the stage, Justin tweeted: 'in DC preparing to sing for President OBAMA!! yeah im nervous. if i mess up he might deport me back to Canada. lol.'

Despite his nerves, he had an amazing time and posted a photo of himself, Usher, the President and Michelle Obama on Twitter for fans to see. He also posted a video on YouTube with the message: 'These past 2 years have been amazing. I have gone from singing in my little town of Stratford to singing the same song, SOMEDAY AT CHRISTMAS by Stevie Wonder, to the President of the United States! It was an incredible honor and I was really nervous. You can tell by my hands, I didn't know what to do with them. I was like Will Ferrell in Talladega Nights. haha. But what I am getting at is that all this has happened thanks to YouTube videos and fans like you. You have all changed my life forever.'

The second time Justin met the Obamas was on 5 April 2010 at the White House Easter Egg Roll. President Obama introduced Justin onstage before he performed to an audience of 30,000 and he accidentally pronounced his surname 'BYE-ber', not 'BEE-ber'. But Justin wasn't offended and he told

People magazine: 'He messed up my name, but I give it to him. He's not [the] age category I sing to. He's not "One Less Lonely Girl".'

Justin tweeted: 'they had snipers and secret service around but the President let 30k people onto the lawn. pretty cool…

'I got to go into the White House and get a tour and a pic with the first family. they are really nice and had a lot of fun but after 3 performances in 90 degree hot sun…Im completely dehydrated and almost passed out after the last one….need to drink some water.

'thanks to everyone who came out today…it was a pretty incredible experience and I am grateful for the honor. Thanks to all the fans.'

Justin has met the Obamas since then, and each time is special to him.

DID YOU KNOW?

In June 2013, Justin and his crew visited Disney World Florida, using underground tunnels and staff entrances to get around. They enjoyed exclusive access to Space Mountain so they could enjoy themselves in peace without being snapped by the paparazzi. Justin and Scooter Braun's families had also been there together in August 2012.

Justin will never forget his eighteenth birthday on 1 March 2012. So many members of his family flew in to celebrate with him in Los Angeles and he enjoyed a special dinner and a party with his nearest and dearest. His brother Jaxon and sister Jazmyn were too young to attend the evening celebrations but he spent time with them during the day. At the party, his manager Scooter had arranged for Justin's celebrity friends Ashley Tisdale, Ryan Good and his girlfriend at the time Selena Gomez to come along and Carly Rae Jepsen performed her hit 'Call Me Baby' just for him. Justin had an unforgettable birthday weekend!

DID YOU KNOW?

Usher and Scooter bought Justin a Fisker Karma sports car for his eighteenth birthday, costing approximately $100,000. Justin was given the car on *The Ellen DeGeneres Show*, with Scooter saying: 'You work really, really hard. I always yell at you don't get anything flashy. You know, we're not about that. Be humble, be humble and I kind of broke my own rule.

'So we wanted to make sure you were environmentally friendly and we wanted to make sure since you love cars that when you're on the road you are always environmentally friendly, and we decided to get you a car that would make you stand out.

'I think you know where I'm going and you're kind of freaking out right now.'

Because Justin is hugely popular in America it's hard for him to walk around unnoticed. Wherever he goes, he is followed by the paparazzi, and if fans find out where he is then he can soon be surrounded by hundreds of screaming girls. Once, when he went out for a meal in New York with Rihanna, he wore a trench coat, hat and sunglasses but he was still recognised by the paparazzi. Whenever he meets up with a female friend, the press love to speculate that they are dating.

If you ever want to send Justin a letter or gift, the address you need is in America. He loves receiving post from fans but can't always get back to everyone. (If you would like an autograph, make sure you include a self-addressed envelope with your letter.)

The address you need is:

Justin Bieber
c/o Island Def Jam Group
Worldwide Plaza

825 8th Ave
28th Floor
New York, NY 10019
USA

Justin thinks Beliebers are simply the best and is thankful for every single fan that supports him. In October 2009, he discussed Beliebers with *Details* magazine. He revealed: 'I met a six-month-old baby. I've got some young fans, but the majority of them are like 14, 15. My mom's like 35, so she's my oldest fan.

'I don't mind it [when fans flash their bras]. Just kidding – it's not something that's cool for them to do. There was this one girl in Seattle – I didn't even see her – she runs at me, tries to give me a hug and tackles me. It was really aggressive and scary.'

Justin doesn't like it when fans fight and, during one performance in Pittsburgh, he had to stop singing mid-song. He had thrown a towel into the audience and two fans had started fighting because they both wanted it.

DID YOU KNOW?

During Justin's World Tour of 2010 and 2011, he performed in 64 cities in America.

Justin has won lots of awards and attends as many award ceremonies as he can but sometimes he just needs a break. At the Teen Choice Awards 2013, he won three awards, but didn't make an appearance at the award ceremony. He did tweet Beliebers, though, saying: '4 years in a row. #tcas. That's love. Thank u. Enjoying the break. But always here. Thank u. This is forever.

'Our story. Our awards. Our songs. Our albums. Our tour. Our journey…just beginning. This is forever. Thank u. Love.'

Justin was thrilled to receive the first ever Milestone Award from CeeLo Green at the Billboard Music Awards in Las Vegas in May 2013. In his acceptance speech, he said: 'I'm nineteen years old – I think I'm doing a pretty good job. Basically, from my heart, I really just want to say, it should really be about the music, it should be about the craft that I'm making. This is not a gimmick. I'm an artist, and I should be taken seriously, and all this other bull should not be spoken of.

'I want to thank my manager Scooter Braun, I want to thank my family at home, I want to thank my mother, my father, I wanna thank Jesus Christ. Momma, I love you so much; Dad, I love you; little brother and sister, I love you so much. Thank you, guys, so much. Fans, you are incredible.'

Justin also picked up the Top Male Artist and Top Socialist Artist awards that night.

DID YOU KNOW?

During Justin's Believe show in Atlanta on 10 August 2013, the girl he serenaded in 'One Less Lonely Girl' was Ludacris' daughter Karma. Her dad tweeted: 'Happy Bday Karma. Daddy Loves you!'

Scooter presented Justin with a Diamond Award during his Believe show in Newark, New Jersey on 31 July 2013. The Diamond Award is given to artists when they have sold 10 million singles or albums. 'Baby' had actually sold 12 million copies, which made it the most sold single ever in America. Justin was over the moon to receive the award and said: 'First and foremost, I want to thank all my Beliebers in the audience tonight. And all my Beliebers at home, and my mom for always believing in me.'

DID YOU KNOW?

When Justin visited Ohio in July 2013, he went to Columbus Zoo and got to cuddle a baby snow leopard.

After Justin's show in Denver, Colorado, Scooter Braun explained how much Justin means to him in a series of tweets. He wrote: 'Very happy tonight. I love this kid. And I have his back forever. @justinbieber is #family and I am proud of him. He is growing and pushing himself as a young man and doing it with the world watching. And what he wants is to be good. To be great. And to mean something positive to the world despite the obstacles or the pressures. His heart is pure and I will be right there with him like I promised him 6 years ago. It is all love. How we react to adversity is what defines us as men. proud of u jb. Great talk. Thank u. Love u man!'

DID YOU KNOW?

After his concert in Atlanta, Georgia in December 2012, Justin gave away his pet hamster to a random fan. She was so grateful and looked after PAC until he passed away in March 2013. The fan, called Tori, tweeted Justin and Alfredo to say: 'thank u guys for what u done for me. Having him was truly a blessing & a small beacon of hope! I love u guys!' Beliebers managed to get #RIPPAC trending on Twitter too!

Occasionally, Justin makes mistakes when he is performing. During his performance of 'Fall' at the San Jose concert on 26 June 2013, he accidentally forgot some of the words. He tweeted afterwards: 'San Jose was right tonight. I might of forgot the words to Fall for a second there. Things happen. Lol.'

Over the years, American fans have staged a number of flash mobs to show Justin just how much he means to them. Videos of the flash mobs are available to view on YouTube. These include a great flash mob and Bieber Parade by Beliebers in El Paso, Texas, which took place on 2 June 2012. The best-ever American flash mob was at Hartsfield-Jackson Atlanta International Airport and involved Justin's dancers. They had been waiting in the airport terminal when their flight was cancelled and so they decided to perform 'Beauty And A Beat'. The crew members who took part were: DJ Tay James, B Harv, Melly Baldwin, Kaili Bright, Christina Chandler, Salemah Gabriel, Elysandra Quinones, Nick DeMoura, Jonathan Rabon, Johnny Erasme, Luke Broadlick and Shaun Evaristo. The other passengers in the airport waiting for their flight couldn't get over how polished the flash mob was and took photos of the dancers. They had no idea they were Justin's actual dancers!

DID YOU KNOW?

On 6 February 2013, Justin became the youngest artist to have had five No. 1 albums in America. He is also one of only nine artists who have had No. 1 albums for four consecutive years.

ANNA'S STORY

Anna is sixteen and from Chicago. Her favourite three songs (at the moment) are 'One Less Lonely Girl', 'Fall' and 'Love Me Like You Do'. She says: 'Being a Belieber in America is fun because he [Justin] comes here often and lives here so he is easier to meet and it is also easier to get tickets to his concerts. I have taken part in events at my school by celebrating his birthday and having a Justin Bieber day when I was in middle school, in addition to concerts, buy-outs [events where fans go to a store and buy all of Justin's CDs to donate to children at a local hospital], and movies.

'I met Justin on 4 May 2010. The night before I had been sitting in my room when a notification popped up that Justin had tweeted "Oprah tomorrow". As I read this, I had a flashback to the previous year, when I had walked past Harpo Studios and a worker had kindly greeted my sister and I, telling us that, if we had come just a few minutes early, we could have gotten into the show on stand-by. With this flashback came a plan: I begged my parents to let me skip school and go to try and get tickets on stand-by, and finally, my dad gave in. The following morning, we drove downtown and there was already a massive line to get inside. Everyone there had tickets, and a worker explained that they were already overcapacity and no one on stand-by was going to be let in. I was extremely disappointed, and my dad gave me the "I told you so" face. The woman in line in front of me was in the same situation, and she came up with the idea to go wait outside the garage to catch a glimpse of him in his car, so we did. Over the next two hours, about five others came. I was starting to lose hope that maybe Justin would go through a different entrance, when a couple of security guards came out and made us step aside.

'A black limo-bus pulled up and, as I glanced through the semi-tinted window, I saw a boy flip his hair: immediately, I knew it was him. The car was going to go into the garage, but Justin made the decision to step out. He was so genuine and nice, taking pictures with every single person there and signing autographs for everyone. He even answered some questions like "What song are you gonna sing?" After a couple minutes, he told us he had to go and I screamed, "Can I please have a hug?!" Justin hugged me as Kenny pulled him away and I swear I will never forget that moment. He walked in and turned around to flash us one last peace sign. He didn't have to get out of the car; he didn't have to talk to us or take pictures. He didn't even have to look at us. But he chose to take a minute to make our day, to make us cry and laugh, because that's just how amazing he is. I love Justin so much, and I'll never forget that amazing day!'

NATALIE'S STORY

Sixteen-year-old Natalie is from New Jersey. Her favourite three songs are 'Believe', 'Never Say Never' and 'One Less Lonely Girl'. She says: 'There are a lot of things I love about Justin. I love his voice and the way he expresses himself through music and I also love how he inspires us Beliebers to follow our dreams. I have attended a *Believe Acoustic* buy-out and I have hosted a food drive inspired by Justin and his crew. They are so inspirational – they teach us that we can make a difference.

'I haven't been fortunate enough to meet Justin yet but I have met Scooter. Here is how it happened: I had been trying to see Justin in concert since 2009 but could never afford tickets. When Believe Tour tickets were announced, I already knew I wasn't going to be able to afford them, so I couldn't buy any. Despite this, I told my friends that I was going to try to find my way into a show. November 28th came and it was the first show at Madison Square Garden. My mom and I had been planning on going to New York that day to see what could happen. I had made a poster that said, "Just an Out Of Town Girl who would Die In Your Arms for some Believe tickets to see my Boyfriend. Never Say Never right?" I was hoping that someone in the Bieber crew might notice and help me.

'My mom and I got to freezing NYC around 3.30pm and went out in the back where the rest of the Beliebers were waiting. While waiting, we saw Dan Kanter and Pattie. Later, Alfredo came out and I thought he was going to give out tickets so I started crying and yelling for him, but all he did was get his friend. At around 7.40pm nothing was happening so my mom was like, "Maybe we should just leave since the show has already started?" I convinced her to stay a little longer and she agreed and went to the entrance of the arena to warm up. (My mom only went inside because I made friends with another girl who was alone and, if we got tickets, my mom said she would give her ticket to the girl.) Then out of nowhere Scooter Braun comes out with tickets! First, he went over to some other fans and then he came to the girl next to me. The whole time I'm just like, "Scooter, please, I'm from New Jersey," but he didn't hear me and gave the group next to me tickets, then he started walking away. Then I started crying hysterically while holding my poster up until a security guard saw me and knew how long I had been waiting.

'The security guard took my poster, showed it to Scooter and that's when Scooter came back to me. I said again, "PLEASE, SCOOTER, I'M FROM NEW JERSEY. I'VE NEVER SEEN JUSTIN BEFORE." Then he asked me, "Who you with?" so I just pointed to the girl next to me and said "her". Then he looked through his tickets and handed me two and said, "You guys are going in together!" I cried 10x harder and yelled "Thank You", and just started to run to the entrance of the arena. The girl and I went to look for my mom and when I got to her, I collapsed onto the floor crying and telling her everything that had just happened. When we got inside to our seats we found out we were on the floor, only three rows from the front! Then the most amazing concert started and, after four years of trying, I finally saw my idol in concert. I just want to say THANK YOU to Scooter because he made my dreams come true that night and DREAMS DO COME TRUE.

'Never Say Never really works so if you have a dream you better work hard for it because they do come true.'

JESSICA'S STORY

Jessica is sixteen and from New York. Her favourite three songs are 'Be Alright', 'Down To Earth' and 'Believe'. If she had to say what she loves about Justin the most, she couldn't. Jessica explains: 'I couldn't explain it with just words but I can honestly say without exaggeration that his music and his general existence gave me the strength and hope to continue living my life. He was always there in spirit during every one of my struggles and provided much-needed inspiration. Being a Belieber in America, and in New York, is simultaneously the most incredible experience yet difficult at the same time. New York has such a big population and the majority of his fans are teenagers, but whenever he comes to visit it usually disrupts the entire wellbeing of the city in the best and worst way. But in a way, it's like we're all one big family and it's the reason I've made so many friend-ships in the process.

'This is the story of when I had met Justin Bieber for the very first time. I heard he'd be in New York to perform on *The Today Show*, so I convinced my mom to camp out with me in the hope of finally seeing him, just once. So we waited and waited regardless of the fact it was pouring rain and really cold. Practically hurricane-like weather and, still, we waited on the sidewalk. I had set up a tent in a thunderstorm just for him (Romantic, eh?) because all I ever wanted was to meet the guy who's been there for me all this time without even knowing who I am. But there got a point where our teeth were chattering, our clothes were soaked like we had been thrown into an ocean and our eyes resembled a raccoon's from all the energy being drained.

'So my mom insisted we should go home. And I remember thinking, "We already made it this far, why stop now?" But I obliged. As we were packing it up... (Plot Twist) we hear a roar of screams and there he was. It was as if the entire world was blurred out and he was the only visible sight. I stared in awe with my face probably red as ever from not only the cold but the blood rushing to my cheeks from the sight of him. He walked down the row of fans, taking time for each of them with security, and finally stood right in front of me. He probably noticed I was too flustered and overwhelmed to speak. So he broke the ice by smiling with a "Hi beautiful!" I was thinking, did he just call me...?

'Hearing his voice in person and not on my iPod made my heart want to beat out of my chest but I managed to stutter a really enthusiastic "Hi" while looking right into his eyes. He flashed such a genuine smile at me and reached out for a high-five. I ended up grasping and holding his hand so tightly for a firm five seconds. While our fingers were still locked together, he said, "Ah, your hands are so cold!" He looked sympathetically at me and leaned in to hug me and that was that.'

KAELYN'S STORY

Sixteen-year-old Kaelyn is from Los Angeles. Her favourite three songs are 'Runaway Love', 'Never Let You Go' and 'Thought Of You'. The things she loves most about Justin are his voice and his eyes. She says: 'His voice has such a perfect tone. I also love his personality – I feel like me and him are already close and I feel like we have been best friends for a long time.

'In my country we are very blessed and I have been able to help a lot of Beliebers in my community. I have been to a buy-out, a Belieber bowling party and soon I will be going to a Belieber party. There are lots of Justin fans in Los Angeles.'

Kaelyn met Justin on 1 September 2012 but her story started three days earlier when she sent a tweet to try to find out where Justin's dance studio was. Thankfully, one of her friends had been there the week before and met Justin, so she sent her a direct message with the address. Kaelyn promised to keep the address to herself so that the studio wouldn't be bombarded with hundreds of Beliebers. She takes up her story: 'I jumped, screamed, and I cried and cried.

Finally I told my mom what happened: I had the address I needed. She was in shock because she never really thought I would find a way to meet Justin, but I had hope. When I asked her if I could go see Justin she said "NO", just a flat-out "NO". As soon as I heard no, I ran into my room crying because I couldn't fully understand why she wouldn't let me go. She came in my room and told me it was because she knows he won't be there, but I knew he would be there, I believed. I had been trying to see him since 2009.

'The next day I went to school and I was so upset and disappointed. I got into an argument with a friend who said, "You will never meet Justin Bieber" and I said, "YES I WILL AND WHEN IT HAPPENS YOU WILL FEEL STUPID." I had to prove my haters wrong, I had to!!! I went home that Friday and asked my mom one more time. She still said no. Then next morning was the day I wanted to meet Justin so I woke up early, hoping for my mom to come in my room and say I was going to the studio. She didn't so I tried one more time and ran into her room and asked sweetly, "May I please go see Justin?" She finally said, "Sure, as long as you pay for the gas to get there and back." I found the money and called my best friend Jasmine as I wanted her to come along too.

'As soon as we arrived at the dance studio my friend Jasmine screamed because she saw Alfredo. We jumped out of the car so fast and ran to Alfredo to ask for a picture before he left. Then we waited for about three hours and then all of a sudden we heard, "Hey, guys, look what I brought you!" I COULDN'T BELIEVE MY EARS!!!! Justin was holding a cake for us and he told us to get in line. The whole time in line I wanted to cry but I couldn't because I didn't want my picture to be ruined. It finally came my turn and I asked him for a kiss on the cheek, but he said, "Can we just take the picture?" and I was like, "Of course." He only said that because he was in a rush and he wanted each fan to get their own individual picture. After my time with Justin I ran over to my mom, crying. She was stood chatting to Kenny. After so many years of contests, helping others out, hoping and wishing, it had finally paid off!'

BRITTANY'S STORY

Eighteen-year-old Brittany is from New York. Her favourite three songs are 'One Time', 'Die In Your Arms' and 'Believe'. She loves how Justin inspires people never to give up on their dreams and thinks that it's great to be a New York Belieber because, when Justin visits, 'Everyone is out and about supporting him, Beliebers never sleep when he is in town.'

Brittany managed to meet Justin on 31 July 2013 in New Jersey with her friends Jessica, Brianna and Dana. She says: 'We told him we loved his tattoos so he held his arm out and we all were looking at his tattoos. He asked which one we liked – I chose his "Believe" tattoo on his inner arm. I couldn't believe we were talking to Justin Bieber. We all had a group hug and it was amazing. He called us "Gorgeous!" We saw Ryan and Chaz too, it was the best day of our lives!'

AMANDA'S STORY

Amanda is sixteen and from Norwalk, Fairfield County. Her favourite three songs are 'Catching Feelings', 'One Time' and 'Be Alright'. She says: 'My favourite thing about Justin is his music. He's obviously gorgeous but his songs always make me feel better. I love it that there are so many Beliebers in America but it means that tickets are so hard to get because so many fans want to see his concerts.

'I love going to buy-outs and, when "Never Say Never" came out, I took part in a flash mob organised by my friends Lauren, Christina, Katelyn and Kylee. We all stood in the shape of Justin's initials and sang "Baby" together – it was a great experience. You can see it on YouTube if you search for "JB Flash mob: Milford, Connecticut". Dan Kanter has seen the video and said he thought it was amazing.

'Meeting Justin has always been a goal of mine but, every time I tried to meet him, I was told he came out five minutes earlier. I was constantly disappointed and I was ready to give up. Every time Justin came to New York, I travelled from Norwalk to try to meet him. It was never even close to successful until this one time. One day, I got an email telling me I won five tickets to see Justin on the music video show *106 & Park*. I didn't remember entering, so I called the studio to make sure it was all legit: it was.

'I arrived at the studio very early. It was so hot – I didn't think I was going to make it because I was feeling ill. The studio workers wouldn't let me sit down, even though I was seconds from passing out. They finally let us inside and I just made it to a chair; it was nicer inside and I started to feel better. They first told us the rules and brought us to the set. We were told Justin wasn't there and this was a wrap-around show. I'm pretty sure everyone in there was worried: we didn't travel all the way there to just be on the show, we wanted to see Justin.

'They came around and gave us another wristband to show that we could come back to see Justin. That show started and Justin finally came out. I couldn't believe he was right there in front of me! He did a short interview and then took pictures with some studio workers and left. We were ready for the show to continue, but Justin came back. He went around each section to shake everyone's hands and give hugs. I had never been this close to Justin before. I was lucky to be on the edge of the bleachers so I got a hug. After he left, my friends and I couldn't help but cry. We had waited three years for that moment.

'Watching the show back, they showed us crying – it was pretty funny! I wish I could have stayed and tried to meet Justin in the city, but it was such a hot day – I couldn't handle it. The next day I went with my friend to see Justin on Fuse TV – it was incredible that we managed to get audience tickets for two shows in two days! It was being filmed in a museum and we thought we were the first there but, after waiting for an hour on our own, we discovered the line was somewhere else so, by the time we joined it, we were right at the back. We ended up getting the last two seats.

'Justin came out and the interview was amazing. I kept getting his attention and I was happier than ever. He was so down-to-earth and funny. At one point during a commercial, I asked for a hug. Justin gave me a look trying to say he can't right now, but in a super-nice way because then they were about to be fixing his make-up and stuff like that. Right when we all thought the show was over, Justin stood up, and so did I. I stood up with open arms and he came right to me and hugged me. It was so much better than the first time because it wasn't just a one-arm hug, it was legit; I told myself that, even though I didn't have a picture with Justin, this was the next best thing.

'The show premiered on 21 July. I watched and I saw myself the whole time right on the side of Justin. At the end they zoomed in on Justin hugging me. It was amazing to be able to have a picture hugging Justin, even though it's kinda blurry. I guess everything that day happened for a reason. If I had my rightful spot in line, I would have been in a different seat, possibly not as close. I'm so grateful for everything that happened that week.'

ISABELLA'S STORY

Isabella is sixteen and from New York. Her favourite three songs are 'U Smile', 'Die In Your Arms' and 'Favorite Girl'. She met Justin on 18 June 2012 when he appeared on the chat show *The View*. Before she went into the TV studio, she met Dan Kanter and DJ Tay James, which she enjoyed, but meeting Justin was a lot more special. She says: 'At first we were sat near the back of the studio but then a member of *The View* crew moved us so we were right at the front. When Justin came out for his interview, I couldn't feel my body – I was going crazy, he was so close!

'When he went on stage to perform "Boyfriend", I

was even closer. When he was singing the line "Girl-friend, girlfriend, you can be my girlfriend", he came to touch my hands and he looked at me in the eyes while he sang! That was the best moment of my life.

'When he sang "Die In Your Arms", it was so beautiful. His face is so perfect and his smile is gorgeous. His voice is so true and amazing, it's breathtaking. During some moments in that song, he would stare at me with those beautiful sparkly hazel eyes. I swear, they're so much better in person than they are on screen or in posters. I couldn't believe I looked into Justin Bieber's eyes in real life! They make you melt, honestly.'

CHAPTER 3

AUSTRALIA

The first time Justin toured Australia was in April 2011 as part of his My World Tour. He performed in Brisbane, Sydney, Melbourne, Adelaide and Perth. He had some time off to hit the beach and play football with his crew. The show received fantastic reviews from both the Beliebers and the critics. Jordana Borensztajn from *Novafm.com.au* wrote in her review of his first performance in Melbourne: 'Opening with "Love Me", the crowd was going mental throughout the entire show. To be completely honest, "Bieber fever" was an understatement. The vibe, electricity and chaos inside Rod Laver Arena was far more than a fleeting feeling that passes. The screams and yells were so loud and so constant it felt like Rod Laver Arena was shaking at its core. It needed to be experienced to "Beliebed".

'Highlight tracks included his Usher collaboration "Somebody To Love", his hopeful documentary anthem, "Never Say Never", his early hit "U Smile", his ballads, "That Should Be Me" and "Down To Earth" and of course, his biggest track to date, "Baby".'

When Justin was about to sing 'Never Say Never', he brought onto the stage Casey Heynes. Casey is a teenager from Sydney, who was for three years tormented by bullies (he became famous after a video of himself turning the tables on a bully was posted on YouTube). Justin thinks Casey is a real-life hero and asked the audience: 'I wanna ask if anyone in here has been bullied before, how many of those people have seen people get bullied?' before Casey appeared. Justin then added, 'I just wanted to say, he is very inspirational, he shows other people to stand up for what they believe in.'

At this point, the audience went wild, clapping and cheering for both Casey and Justin.

For Justin's Believe Tour, he performed in the same cities again, during November and December 2013. In fact, his last concert of the Believe Tour was on 8 December in Perth.

When Justin visited Australia for the first time, he

was bombarded with so many fans, he jokes that he 'almost died' in the airport. He says he will never forget what happened. His security team decided that for his second visit he should get in a car as soon as he could and then they would drive him out through a back exit to make sure he was safe. Some fans were disappointed, but word soon got around which hotel he was staying in and so they headed there and sang outside all night.

DID YOU KNOW?

Justin's grandparents, Diane and Bruce Dale, came with him when he visited Australia for the first time.

On 18 July 2012, Justin performed on the final of *Australia's Got Talent*. He sang 'As Long As You Love Me' and 'Boyfriend'. Afterwards, he received a standing ovation and fans screamed continuously as he was interviewed. The night before, he had reached 25 million followers on Twitter so he was feeling super-happy. Shortly before he left the stage, a fan ran up to him and he gave her a hug before security led her away. He was only in Australia for three days to promote his album *Believe*, so he had lots of interviews lined up.

When interviewed by Sunrise Australia, he admitted that one artist with whom he would love to collaborate and hasn't yet is Beyoncé. He also said: 'With my music I always like to give inspiring messages – you know, I have a platform to do so much good. I feel I have to use this, so with my album I named it *Believe* just because there are so many people that have struggles and that might want to give up; you should never give up. Never give up, never say never!'

DID YOU KNOW?

Justin likes it when fans wait for him outside his hotel. If there are no fans outside, he finds it strange – he likes knowing there are fans just a short distance away. When it is very cold or raining, he feels sorry for the fans outside and wishes they would go home and come back the next day instead. Justin loves and cares for all of his fans so much and doesn't want anyone to make themselves ill.

Australian Beliebers are extremely dedicated. In early July 2012, a small group of fans decided to do a flash mob outside the studios of Sunrise, Today FM and

Smallzy in Sydney to show everyone just how excited they were that Justin would soon be arriving in Australia. Sunrise actually interviewed some of Australia's biggest Beliebers, and asked what it is they love about Justin. Superfan Katherine Willow replied: 'Everything – he's so great, he's good-looking and I love his voice.'

Ruby Spence became a fan after hearing his music for the first time and Paris Knite revealed that it is the fact that he is really inspirational that made her become a Belieber. The two girls saw Justin in a car and he waved to them. They had been planning on seeing Justin perform at the Overseas Passenger Terminal at Sydney's Circular Quay but the show was cancelled after things got out of hand. Over 4,000 Beliebers had decided to camp the night before to make sure they got a good spot. Things went a bit crazy at 2am when a rumour went round that Justin was already there. The local police tried their best to control the situation but, with so many fans, it was inevitable some would suffer minor injuries. In the end, the show had to be cancelled and the Beliebers were forced to make their way home. Justin was upset and tweeted: 'I love my fans and I am just as disappointed as everyone else with the news from this morning. I want to sing for my fans.'

SOPHIE'S STORY

Sophie is nineteen and from Iluka, New South Wales. Her favourite three songs are 'One Less Lonely Girl', 'Born To Be Somebody' and 'Love Me'. She says: 'What I love about Justin the most is that he is always working hard for us Beliebers. When he is meant to be on break, he is in the studio recording new music for us. He is so down-to-earth.

'Being an Australian Belieber is amazing because there are so many teams and parades organised for Justin, so he has so much support and so much love from his Beliebers here in Australia. I am the leader of Perth Bieber Team in Australia so I host many events and parades for Justin here in Perth. We raise money for sick kids, hold Bieber buy-out events and have screenings of *Never Say Never* for the Perth Beliebers.

'I have been supporting Justin for three to four years now and I seriously don't know what I would be doing with my life right now if it wasn't for Justin. I always knew that I would meet Justin; even if it took ten years, I would. I always got bullied for supporting him and always got told that, "You're never going to meet him, Sophie", "He will never know you exist, so just stop!", "Step into reality and stop telling everyone you're going to meet him because you're not!" But the thing is, I always used to laugh and say, "Ha ha, okay, people, okay. You watch, I'll prove you wrong one day!" and guess what? I DID, TWICE.

'On 25 May 2012, my friend Summer and I both received an email from Bieberfever.com telling us about the new North America tour dates for the Believe Tour and we both just looked at each other as if to say, GET THE LAPTOPS! Even though we are from Australia, we were committed to fly all the way from Australia to New York to see Justin. We told our parents about it and they thought it was amazing that we were so dedicated to him to fly twenty-five hours to see him. I think our parents thought that we didn't have a chance to get tickets because we ALL knew how quickly they were going to go, but it was worth a shot. We looked at the tickets and the prices and saw that there were Meet & Greet tickets available and we cried: they were the tickets we wanted.

'So the tickets came on sale at 12am Perth, Australia time and we had four to five laptops set up with about ten links to each concert; we were so nervous it made us feel sick to the stomach. As soon as it was 12, my laptop went SO SLOW and all the links kept freezing and some even put me in a queue to get the tickets, and it actually made me upset that, if I missed out on tickets for America, I might miss out when he comes to Australia. Every website kept telling us that it was sold out and all the tickets were gone, and we were pretty devastated until Summer just screamed so loud, "I GOT THEM, I GOT THEM, I GOT THEM, I GOT THEM!" I have never gotten out of a chair so quickly in my life and ran over to Summer's laptop and said, "WHAT ONES? MEET & GREET?" We didn't even care what tickets we had, we just wanted to go SO BADLY.

'After buying whatever tickets we were buying we saw the confirmed page and it said:

Justin Bieber – Believe Tour
12th November 2012 – 7:30pm
Barclays Center, Brooklyn NY
2x Meet & Greet Experience
Total: $906.00

'I have never screamed so much in my life. I just remember turning to my mum and saying, "She got Meet & Greet!" and my mum said, "She got it", and me and Summer went CRAZYYYYYYY! My mum was pretty much going crazy with us.

'So that was it – we were MEETING Justin Bieber in NEW YORK in November and NO ONE was taking that away from us. Well that's what we thought, until Summer told me that her parents weren't very happy with her going, so Summer had to make the decision to not go, and it was really, really upsetting. I felt really bad for Summer because she got the tickets and she couldn't go, and if it wasn't for her, I wouldn't be going to meet Justin. I had to find someone who would come with me to New York to meet Justin, and I knew in my head who I would ask: Lauren. I was a bit shaken to call her and ask her, because of the whole meeting Justin thing and we hadn't spoken in about two to three months. She ended up saying yes and we fixed everything, and that was it: she was coming to New York to meet Justin with me.

'Before I left to go to New York, I was on *Bieberfever.com*, just looking at the forum posts, etc., and I saw that there was a contest and all you had to do was send in a photo of all your Bieber things and put it into a collection. So I thought, well, I am already meeting Justin but I do want to send in a photo, so I did.

'The day before the concert, we went to Justin's hotel to hopefully get a glimpse of him walking out or in his car. We saw Scrappy outside and we had a good chat with him; we told him we were from Australia and we started talking about the My World Tour in Australia and when they were coming back. We waited for twelve hours, and, as soon as his car came out, I saw his window go down and the car stop where Justin was, RIGHT IN FRONT OF ME. I got a photo with him and I couldn't have been happier. It was so amazing of him to stop because there were quite a few fans outside the hotel as well, but he did.

'We got to New York and it's such a beautiful city. We woke up on 12 November and that was the day of Justin's concert. I checked my emails and found out that I had won two Meet & Greet tickets for that night. I cried and my heart was beating so fast. Even though we already had Meet & Greets, all I could think was, "What am I going to do with them?" I went up to two young girls at the arena and said, "Have you got tickets to the show?" They looked a bit confused but replied, "Yes, yes, we do! Why?" I told them, "I won two Meet & Greet passes for Justin Bieber and I already have Meet & Greet tickets. Would you like them?" It was honestly the most amazing thing I have ever heard/seen. One of the girls started to cry while the other one screamed, "ARE YOU LYING? PLEASE DON'T LIE," and then when I insisted I was telling the truth, they just kept saying, "OH MY GOSH, THANK YOU SO MUCH, THIS MEANS SO MUCH."

'After the show, Lauren and I got interviewed by some documentary people outside. We got filmed for about ten minutes – they were asking us questions about how long it took to get to New York, how much we love Justin, why we love him, etc. It was a great way to end an AMAZING night. Scrappy even remembered us and came up and said hello and took a photo, along with Adam and Dan!

'I love helping Beliebers meet Justin, that's why giving the Meet & Greets I won to those two girls just made me feel even better that I had made two girls' dreams come true. I try to help as many Beliebers as I can to meet Justin and try to get noticed, even if it's them getting noticed on Twitter. I feel so privileged to have met Justin and want every Belieber to experience the same. I am going to every show for the Australian leg of the "Believe" Tour – I can't wait!'

CHAPTER 4

AUSTRIA

Justin didn't perform his My World Tour in Austria but he did perform his Believe Tour in Vienna on 30 March 2013, much to the delight of Austrian Beliebers. They had been waiting years to see him perform live.

When Justin arrived in Austria, he was thrilled to see so many fans waiting outside his hotel. He tweeted: 'Love to all the fans outside! That was crazy. Post the pics so I can see them. Get ready for the show! #vienna #BELIEVEtour

'My Beliebers in Vienna! Love you!'

To see a short video of Justin signing autographs outside the hotel, search on YouTube for 'Justin Bieber & Fans Vienna, Austria'.

After the show, Justin and his crew went to a club but they ended up being banned after his security team were allegedly too rowdy. Club manager Joachim Bankel told *The Austrian Times*: 'Justin Bieber is no longer welcome here.' Fans were disappointed because it wasn't Justin who had misbehaved and he was leaving for Germany the next day anyway.

If you are an Austrian Belieber, you should become a fan of Justin Bieber Austria Official on Facebook to find out about future fan events and news.

ANNA'S STORY

Sixteen-year-old Anna is from Sankt Veit an der Glan. Her favourite three songs are 'One Less Lonely Girl', 'Pray' and 'Be Alright'. Anna is the only Belieber in her town but she likes taking part in Bieber fan events in Vienna. When the Madame Tussauds' waxwork of Justin arrived in the city, Anna took part in a flash mob to 'All Around The World', choreographed by Alamande Belfor, one of the judges on *Austria's Next Top Model*.

She says: 'My best friend and I waited for a long time for Justin to have a concert in Austria. One day, I was listening to the radio and they said that Justin was coming here for the "Believe" Tour. I was so happy. My friend's dad ordered the tickets for us. We were both happy every single day until the day of the show came, 30 March 2013.

'When the concert started, I was having so much fun – I just enjoyed every second of it. In front of me there were a lot of security guards. Suddenly, I saw a woman walking around for a couple of minutes. Then I saw the same woman right in front of me. She asked, "How old are you?" "Fifteen," I replied. Then she said, "Do you wanna be the One Less Lonely Girl?" I couldn't believe it was happening to me. I said, "YES, YES, OF COURSE!" I was so shocked, so happy, and it was unbelievable: there were thousands of fans watching the show and she had chosen me. Security took me over the fence, and Jenn [from Justin's crew] took me behind the stage. They gave me a T-shirt and then Kenny [Hamilton] came. I asked him if I could have a picture with him, so we took one quickly. I was waiting behind the curtain until the dancers came and they were holding my crown. My stomach was hurting so much, I was so excited; my heart was beating so fast.

'When the curtain started moving I knew it was my time, and the dancers took me onto the stage. I could barely breathe. I saw Justin and he looked at me. I'll never forget that feeling. He lifted his hand and touched my hair and my face. When the song ended, he asked my name and I replied with "Anna". We then walked together to the backstage area and everything was over. This was the best day of my whole life.'

CHAPTER 5

BELARUS

Justin has fans in so many different countries, even countries he has never visited before. Belarus is a small country bordered by Russia, Ukraine, Poland, Lithuania and Latvia. Belarus Beliebers are very passionate and travel long distances to see Justin perform live. If you are a Belieber from Belarus, you should follow @jbfansbelarus on Twitter to find out the latest news on Justin and learn about future fan events.

Belarus Beliebers would love it if Justin visited them one day, even if it was just for an hour or two. Superfan Anastasiya says: 'It is kinda difficult to be a Belieber in my country. We can't buy Justin's fragrances, books or CDs. Justin has never visited here and I bet he doesn't know that my country exists. We have no magazines with huge posters of Justin inside and stuff like this. But I have found out a way to make it all better: I work a lot, saving money, travelling for Justin's tour, driving to other countries to buy books or fragrances. I will never give up on him.'

Thirteen-year-old Dian from Brest has been bullied for being a Belieber but she will never stop being a fan of Justin. She has been a fan since she was eight years old and says: 'I love everything about Justin – his songs are amazing, especially "Believe", "As Long As You Love Me" and "One Less Lonely Girl".'

Fifteen-year-old Kate from Slonim has been a Belieber for six months but wishes she had heard Justin's music sooner. She says: 'I can't decide what I like about Justin the most, he's just perfect. I wish I could walk into a shop in Belarus and buy a Justin T-shirt but that is impossible because we can't buy his merchandise over here.'

Sixteen-year-old Valery from Minsk loves how Justin's dream came true and hopes that one day her dream of Justin visiting Belarus will come true because she would love to meet him. She adds: 'It would be great to see his smile in real life and to hear him sing "Somebody To Love" live.'

Justin knows that some fans get very nervous when

they meet him and he would like to offer them some advice. He told *Teen Vogue* he would like to say to them: 'Just talk to me, ask me how I'm doing; introduce yourself instead of yelling, "Justin! Justin! Justin! Can I have a picture?" And don't come up to me while I'm eating. How would you like it if I came into your house and started taking pictures of you while you were eating? I hate that!'

DID YOU KNOW?

Justin is super-competitive and loves beating his crew at a game of table tennis.

ANASTASIYA'S STORY

Eighteen-year-old Anastasiya is from Minsk. Her favourite three songs are 'Up', 'Never Let You Go' and 'Be Alright'. In her spare time Anastasiya is a budding songwriter and has set up a tumblr account to share her songs. Check them out by visiting: *http://mybieberhallelujah.tumblr.com*. She has been writing songs for four years and Justin is her main inspiration. Her dream is for Justin to use one of her songs in the future.

Anastasiya reveals: 'I am constantly writing to different record labels and music groups and I have written thousands of letters to producers all over the world – Ellen DeGeneres, Kuk Harrell, Oprah, Justin, Justin's grandparents, Pattie Mallette, Scooter Braun, Mike Posner, and so on – telling them my story and my dream. I hope one day my dream will become reality.'

The first time Anastasiya met Justin was in Berlin, after her dad drove her for twenty-four hours to be there. It was 31 March 2013. While there, she found out that she had won a contest to meet Justin and invited one of her Twitter friends to accompany her. She explains: 'I had been chatting to this girl from Germany for a couple of weeks and she had been so kind to me that I knew I had to invite her to come along too. So I called Adrianna and I was like, "You know what? We're going to attend the Meet & Greet with Justin tomorrow, you and me." She was freaking out even more than me. Seriously. It meant such a lot to know that I made her dream come true – that was such a precious moment I'll never forget.

'On the day of the concert, we were so excited, we couldn't breathe; I woke up really early that day, and my dad drove me to the centre of Berlin – to the Brandenburg Gate. That was the place where me, Adrianna and her friend Katinia met up for the first time. We had about three hours to kill so we went from hotel to hotel, looking for Justin. Adrianna thought she saw his big black bus but it soon disappeared. We met some amazing Beliebers from Denmark called Victoria and Maria. After going into a Dunkin' Donuts to check our Twitter feeds, we read that Justin was on his way to the arena so we all ran as fast as we could to the Metro station. When we arrived at the arena, we were surprised that there weren't many people there. We went to the parking lot gates and saw two huge black "Beet the street" buses – we knew then that Justin was in the house. We started to sing songs with the other Beliebers and Adrianna saw Kenny [Hamilton].

'As we waited, it was freezing cold – there was lots of snow and the wind was howling. We met some more Beliebers from Germany and then we saw Nick, Justin's choreographer. I called out to him and he looked at me and waved. Later, I saw Elysandra [Quiñones] – one of Justin's dancers. When we went inside we had an hour or so to wait, but at least it was warm. We saw Kenny and then it was finally our turn to meet Justin. Me and Adrianna were shaking; we were standing near the curtains. I saw Dustin and Mikey [Justin's bodyguards] inside the curtains and then I saw Justin from his back. I wanted to scream so much, but I knew I couldn't. After we walked in, I stood for a moment in shock with my mouth opened so wide. And then Justin winked at me and smiled. I swear, that moment I thought I would faint. There are no words to describe how it felt. (And by the way, Justin is so short, like I never expected him to be like that.)

'I went to stand near the little girls we had to share the picture with because we were Meet & Greet winners. I didn't get to stand right next to Justin only because I froze for a moment and the other girls came to him. When the photographer said, "Are you ready?" I found myself looking at Alfredo, not at the camera. And I was smiling like an idiot at him, and then he looked at me and giggled. But then it hit me: I should be looking at the camera, so I did. When it was time for me to go, I walked up to Alfredo and was like, "Hi, Fredo! I have these letters for you!" And I gave him a couple letters that I had written for the Bieber crew. And he was like, "Oh, thank you!" He looked so tired but so sweet at the same time. Then when I was about to leave, I called for Justin, I was like, "Justin! Justin!" But he was too busy discussing something with his bodyguard, Dustin.

'The next day my Twitter mentions exploded – I was just like, "What is happening?" And then I saw that Alfredo, Kenny and Dan had tweeted me about the letters. It was so amazing, I couldn't breathe; my dad was super-excited for me too. I screamed so much, but I cried even more: I had written the letters straight from my heart.'

What the tweets said:

Kenny's tweet: 'Thank you for the letter. It really touched my heart! You are a special person. God bless.'

Alfredo's tweet: 'Thank u for that letter. Sweet.'

Dan's tweet: 'Thank you Anastasia for your kind letter. It was very sweet.'

Anastasiya met Justin for the second time in Russia after her dad drove them there – it took them twelve hours to get to St Petersburg. Anastasia's dad is a huge Justin fan too, so he doesn't mind driving her around Europe to meet him. During their journey, Anastasia received an email saying she had won a Meet & Greet so they were both super-excited. On arrival at the venue, Anastasiya met Ryan Butler and told him she had a special book containing letters from seventy fans, who had asked her to pass them on to Justin. Ryan was really impressed at Anastasiya's dedication because she had travelled so far and thought that she was kind to bring all the letters. He gave her a guitar pick and said he would make sure she got an individual photo with Justin. Anastasiya couldn't believe it and was so shocked when she was ushered into a room, and found Justin standing there in a green jacket. She couldn't help but stare and forgot to look at the cameraman at first.

Anastasiya adds: 'I feel really blessed to have met Justin twice. He was so perfect and I hope to meet him again one day. I loved meeting Ryan too – he was so kind and I am glad I got to give him lots of hugs!'

CHAPTER 6

BELGIUM

Justin loves visiting Belgium. He performed his My World Tour in Antwerp on 30 March 2011 and his Believe Tour on 10 and 11 April 2013. While taking part in a press conference for 'Believe', he told the Belgian press how he stays grounded. He said: 'It's all [about] who you surround yourself with and it's about the people that you know help you grow up, help you become a good person, and I think as long as you keep good people around you, and always have good morals, and know what's wrong and know your boundaries.'

When interviewed by Belgian TV presenter Sean Dhondt, he revealed that he loves comedy movies, especially those starring Adam Sandler, Will Ferrell or

Martin Lawrence. He also said that when he goes to bed at night he thinks about ways he can better his shows, and anything he might have forgotten to do that day. Justin really wishes he could spend more time in Belgium to explore but his schedule is always so packed, he doesn't get the chance.

If you are a Belgian Belieber, you should become a fan of 'Justin Bieber Belgium' on Facebook or join the Netlog social network for JustinBieberOfficial. You should also check out the great fan videos that fans have posted on YouTube.

DID YOU KNOW?

During his trip to Belgium in April 2013, Justin met his look-a-like Robin Verrecas and shook his hand.

MAITÈ'S STORY

Maitè is nineteen and from Ostend. Her favourite three songs are 'Common Denominator', 'Nothing Like Us' and 'Love Me Like You Do'. She says: 'Being a Belieber in my country is not that fun because Justin only comes here once every few years. But when he comes to my country, all the Belgian Beliebers on Twitter who are going to the concert try to meet up at a place so we can go to the arena together and have fun while waiting. We're like a family – we all support that one boy who inspired us. So it's fun.'

She met Justin, Dan Kanter and Kenny Hamilton on 10 April 2013. When she met Dan, he told her he was very excited to be in Belgium and that Justin might have a surprise for the show. She thought he was so sweet and funny! Justin was wearing a snapback. Maitè says: 'He's even more perfect in real life! I went over to Justin and I couldn't believe I was standing next to THE Justin Bieber, it felt so unreal. After the picture was taken, I just froze and kept standing next to him. He grabbed me so tight to him and gave me a side hug; it's such an amazing feeling. I quickly turned around to take one last look at Justin. I was shaking, and started crying.

'Later on, the show started and it was just perfect! We held up signs saying, "We will forever love you as long as you love us" and Justin said to the crowd: "I will forever love you too." We also threw balloons in the air and Justin was so impressed, he just stood there for about seven minutes, looking into the crowd tearing up! I also went to the show on April 11th. I was second row and, again, Justin put on an amazing show. These were the best two days of my life.'

STEFFI'S STORY

Sixteen-year-old Steffi is from Bocholt. She has been a Belieber since 2009. Her favourite three songs are 'Take You', 'Born To Be Somebody' and 'All Around The World'. She finds it hard being a Belgian Belieber because they have to wait longer for songs and albums to be released than American fans and there are not so many competitions for fans to enter.

Steffi met Justin at the Sportpaleis Antwerpen on 10 April 2013. She explains: 'I waited for Justin to come to my country for two years and I couldn't have been any happier when they announced the tour dates for the My World Tour. Turns out the Belgium concert was on the day I had exams so my mom said I couldn't go. I broke down crying and didn't talk to my mom for two days or so. Time passed and I continued to be a Belieber. When I heard Justin was coming back to Belgium, I freaked out! Nobody was going to stop me from going this time!

'A few days before the concert, there was a contest at the local radio station for a Meet & Greet with Justin. I freaked out and tried my best. I got into the final round but I got the last question wrong. I cried so hard, and I talked to the girl who won the contest (@BeliebInDaBieb_). She was really nice and I was happy for her, but I was still so jealous! The day before the concert I was checking Twitter, but then my mentions were blowing up. The girl who won the contest tweeted me, saying: "Check your DM's." I was so confused. She gave me her number, so I called her. "I won another Meet & Greet and I want you to have it! You deserve this!" My world stopped, I couldn't move! I was going to meet Justin Bieber on April 10th.'

On the day itself, Steffi met Dan Kanter first before meeting Justin, alongside four other competition winners. She says: 'I really can't describe the feeling I had. I was the first one to go in, and there he was: Justin Drew Bieber. I couldn't believe it was finally happening! He was wearing sunglasses, but I really wanted to see his gorgeous eyes. I stood next to him and he put his arm around my waist! Just thinking back to that moment makes me go crazy! I also put my arm around his waist. It felt so right! When the picture was taken, we all said that we loved him. He grabbed my shoulder and said, "Thank you so much, I really appreciate it!"

'Before we could say something else, the security guards dragged us out. Then all the emotions came. I was crying so hard, my biggest dream came true! Finally people would stop saying: "You'll never meet him". I went inside the arena, back to my friends and cried in their arms. When the concert started, I realised I was almost right in front of the stage!

Justin came out – I couldn't control myself anymore, I cried so hard. The concert was amazing! I went home so happy!'

KLARA'S STORY

Seventeen-year-old Klara is from Ardooie. Her favourite three songs are 'Never Let You Go', 'Fall' and 'Out Of Town Girl'. She says: 'Being a Belieber in Belgium is kind of hard, because we rarely get any merchandise and Justin has only been here once. However, I am very proud of my country. He won't forget us, of that I am sure, and I couldn't be more proud. There aren't many Beliebers where I live, but I met some amazing Beliebers from other towns at the "Believe" Tour, with whom I still meet up – they've become friends for life.

'I take part in Justin projects in my country. Together with some friends I helped organise a project to hold up paper sheets that read "We will love you forever, as long as you love us" during as "Long As You Love Me" (we also held up balloons during "Believe", which was magical). We haven't had any huge promotional events yet; however, we now have the project #promobelieve3DinBelgium, which is getting bigger and bigger every day. Basically, it's Belgian Beliebers trying to get him back here, we already have gotten international radio stations to help us and we're planning meet-ups with Belgian Beliebers to make a promotion-movie.

'When I met Justin backstage our time together was really rushed but it was still great and I hope to meet him again one day. The concert itself was amazing! You could tell by the sound of his voice that he was a little sick, but that didn't keep him from performing as if his life depended on it. He joked around when bras were being thrown onstage. He also had the biggest smile on his face when he saw our "We will love you forever, as long as you love us" sheets and told us, "I will love you forever as well" – it was the most special moment. He still had to perform "Baby", but he just stood there. He stood at the end of the catwalk and looked at us for ten minutes straight.

'We screamed our lungs out and I've never seen him any happier. His jaw dropped in awe, you could see his lips form the words "Wow!" and "I love you". It was a moment between us, Beliebers and Justin. I have no words for how I was feeling in that moment. I am so proud of our small country. I am so grateful because he took the time to travel to our small country, and spent two nights performing for us.'

CHAPTER 7

BRAZIL

In October 2011, Justin performed his My World Tour in Brazil. He performed in Rio de Janeiro on 5 and 6 October, São Paulo on 8 and 9 October, and Porto Alegre on the 10th. In November 2013, he performed his Believe Tour, performing in São Paulo on 2 November and Rio de Janeiro on the 4th.

One of Justin's most difficult interviews happened when he was in Brazil, being interviewed by a TV host called Sabrina Sato. She couldn't speak English and Justin can't speak Portuguese so the whole interview was very awkward because neither of them could understand what the other one was saying. Sabrina is a comedienne as well as a presenter so the interview did have funny elements to it. Justin admitted he likes

Brazilian girls and thinks they are beautiful. He also revealed he can play the piano, guitar, drums and trumpet before Sabrina presented him with a berimbau to try. A berimbau is a musical bow, with a single string, and Justin had a good attempt at playing it during the interview. To see for yourself, check out the interview on YouTube.

When Justin was visiting Brazil as part of his My World Tour, he was invited to play golf at a special course in São Paulo. He had a great time with his crew but had to borrow some golf clubs since he hadn't brought any on tour with him. Justin loves visiting Brazil and, because it was one of the last destinations on his World Tour, he arranged a surprise party for the crew in a nightclub.

When Brazilian magazine *Todateen* decided to feature Justin on their cover, they chose a very strange photograph, hated by fans in Brazil and worldwide. Fans thought that the magazine had added lipstick and eye shadow to Justin's face in postproduction. So many fans tweeted their disgust that the magazine decided to release a statement to the *Huffington Post*. Translated from Portuguese to English, their statement reads:

We could not help noticing your comments and tweets from the picture of Justin on the magazine's cover. We would like to say there was no change made in the area of the singer's eyes. We had a technical problem that darkens certain areas of the photo.

We also want to say that all of us find Justin very naturally beautiful. We'd never think it necessary to alter pictures of him. Natural beauty says it all, right?

It wasn't the first time that a magazine had portrayed Justin in an unusual way. One magazine cover for *People* magazine even upset Justin himself. On the cover of the American publication, Justin is laughing but he didn't like the angle they had chosen one bit. He tweeted: 'Dear @peoplemag Covershoot...next time i laugh real crazy warn me u r still taking pics...still appreciate u but let's get on the same page.'

The message was soon deleted and replaced with one that said: 'EXCLUSIVE story and pics in the new issue of @peoplemag. I look crazy as heck on the cover but if u cant laugh at yourself u aint havin fun.'

Brazilian Beliebers have set up their own fan site for Justin – *Bieberfeverbrasil.com* – with the latest news as well as some great photos of Justin in Brazil and around the world.

CHAPTER 8

CANADA

For Justin, Canada will always be home and he will never forget his roots. He will always do his best to help fellow Canadians who want to make it in the music business and he tries to visit home as much as he can. He might enjoy visiting beaches when he visits hot countries, but he does like being home in the snow too.

When the UK struggled to cope with a few inches of snow in January 2010, Justin was shocked and told *Digital Spy*: 'You guys are acting like it's the end of the world – everything's cancelled and the subway's not working – but in Canada this is, like, the least amount of snow we get. We have to have at least 10' of snow to get a day off school.'

He also had some advice for people, saying: 'You guys aren't wearing the right sort of clothes – you need to wear hats, scarves, mitts and long johns! I always wear long johns when it's cold. I know they're not cool but I'd rather be warm than cold.'

When journalist Tim Aylen asked Justin which country has the most vocal fans, he replied: 'I think my home country, Canada, has the most vocal fans. It feels unbelievable when I go home to feel such love. It's amazing whenever I get that kind of support, but to be able to connect with my fellow Canadians is awesome!'

Justin grew up in a small town called Stratford in Ontario. It is a quaint, beautiful place and in 1997 was named the Prettiest City in the World by *Nations in Bloom*. Stratford's tourism website boasts: 'We are a charming Victorian city nestled in pastoral country-side a few short hours from Toronto and the U.S. – a destination internationally renowned as one of North America's great arts towns'.

Stratford is a town with a lot of culture; it has an annual Shakespeare festival that draws in lots of visitors. Growing up, Justin didn't much care for the playwright William Shakespeare, but he did like it when theatregoers threw money into his guitar case as he busked outside the Avon Theatre. He was only twelve when he started, but he really wanted to go golfing with his friends so he needed the money – and he liked performing too. On the first day, he managed to raise almost $200 so he decided he would keep busking, and thought that by the end of the summer he might be able to visit Disney World with his mom.

The theatregoers thought that Justin was very talented and were impressed by the range of songs he could do. He sang Christian songs, classic tracks and modern pop songs... something for everyone. Justin told *Rolling Stone Magazine*: 'I sang "I'll Be" by Edwin McCain, "You And Me" by Lifehouse, "U Got It Bad" by Usher and "Cry Me A River" by Justin Timberlake.' He also liked to sing 'Refine Me' by Jennifer Knapp.

Mom Pattie was so proud of Justin that she had recorded him singing at a talent show and put the videos up on YouTube for all to see. Some schoolgirls on a trip to Stratford took a video of Justin singing outside the theatre and posted it on YouTube. For the first time, he started to have fans.

The house manager for the Avon Theatre, Eldon Gammon, told the *Star* newspaper he can remember Justin singing outside: he was the 'little guy with the big voice'. He admitted: 'It almost seemed like the guitar was bigger than him. Student groups, they poured around him. The five-minute call would go – it's an announcement that you could hear all over – and then we would have to drag them away from him. He had a good persona with people. He was always very polite, always said "Thank you". It's interesting that the music he's doing now is nothing like what he did here.'

Justin was raised by his mom and grandparents, as his dad moved far away to Winnipeg, Manitoba, when he was a baby. Money was tight but Justin received lots of love. His mom worked so hard in a number of part-time office roles to make sure he had everything he needed, but they couldn't afford luxuries or holidays. Justin chatted to *Macleans.ca* about his childhood. He said: 'Some people have it misconstrued. I wasn't poor, I definitely didn't think of myself as not having a lot of money but I definitely did not have a lot of money. I couldn't afford to get a lot of new clothes a lot of times but I had a roof over my head. I was very fortunate: I had my grandparents, I saw them a lot, they were very kind. So I grew up getting everything that I wanted.'

DID YOU KNOW?

Justin and his mom Pattie had to say goodbye to their home and Canada once Justin signed to Def Jam Music Group as manager Scooter Braun needed them to move 689 miles away to Atlanta, Georgia in the USA. Justin's grandparents and the remainder of his extended family stayed in Stratford so he didn't have to say goodbye permanently.

People from Justin's hometown are so proud of him that they have created a special Bieber map for Beliebers who visit Stratford, Ontario. If you want to find the different places in Stratford that Justin visited regularly and had a big impact on him, just visit: *www.visitstratford.ca*.

Places to visit in Stratford:

The Avon Theatre – Where Justin busked.

Stratford Skate Park – Justin loved hanging out here with his friends.

Kiwanis Community Centre – The place where Justin entered a talent competition.

Jeann Sauve Catholic School, Stratford Northwestern Public School and Stratford Northwestern Secondary School – Justin's old schools.

Madelyn's Diner – Pattie's favourite restaurant.

Scoopers – Justin and his friends would come here to eat yoghurt cones after their football games.

City Hall – Justin took part in a charity CD launch concert here. You can see his version of 'Set A Place at Your Table' on YouTube.

Features Restaurant – Justin liked having breakfast here as a treat.

William Allman Memorial Arena – Justin played hockey here.

The Pour House (used to be called Sid's Pub) – Justin and his friends loved playing pool here.

Long & McQuade Music Shop – Justin's favourite music shop.

Cooper Standard Soccer Fields – The Stratford Strikers played their matches here.

Should you decide to visit Stratford, make sure you look out for Justin's grandparents, Diane and Bruce Dale, and his friends, Chaz Somers and Ryan Butler. If you ever write to Justin without using his fan mail address, then your letter might end up going to his grandparents' house instead. A spokesperson from Canada Post explained to the *Star* newspaper: 'He's getting maybe a couple pieces of mail a week. It's coming to "Justin Bieber, Stratford, Canada" or "Stratford, Ontario."

'That is not a correct address, but these are interesting circumstances and heck, we have some cognizance of the pop culture at Canada Post, along with everybody else and so do our employees... because of the size of the community, we have an idea who is who – a pop icon who is from this part of the country, with known relatives; we're playing along a little bit for this one.'

Justin has had many special times in Canada, both as a performer and on a personal level. He will never forget his first mini-tour, which happened in early 2009. He was asked by the Canadian clothing retailer Urban Behavior if he would perform at the Urban Behavior store in Vancouver on 1 November, and then at the Edmonton, Montreal, London (the Canadian city) and Toronto stores. For Justin, it was a dream come true. As well as performing in each store, he signed Urban Behavior T-shirts and had photos taken with fans.

Sadly, Justin couldn't be at the first show because he was ill but he made all the other dates. The Toronto show must have been emotional because it was his last one. After his show at the Urban Behavior store wrapped, he headed to the club Kool Haus and performed again. There were so many Beliebers in the audience that Justin must have been buzzing as they cheered and chanted, 'We love you, Justin!'

He performed 'Bigger', 'One Less Lonely Girl', an acoustic version of 'Favourite Girl' and finished his set with Chris Brown's 'With You', telling the crowd:

'This has been like a cool rollercoaster ride, thanks to crowds like you guys.'

Justin was so happy when the My World Tour was announced in March 2010, with 85 dates in America and Canada. It was just a shame that the first dates were in America, not Canada. His first Canadian date was in Toronto on 21 August 2010. Back then, he had no idea that the tour would end up being 130 dates around the world, including Europe, Asia, Oceania and South America.

Justin had been spending some time in Stratford shortly before the tour began so it was hard for him to leave. He tweeted on 21 June: 'Canada thank u!! Sad I had 2 leave but we r starting the tour and had to get back to rehearsals....MY BUS RULES!! It's a party on wheels!'

Performing his first My World Tour was a lot more daunting than the opening night of his mini-tour. So many people were watching to see how well he did. He didn't want to let the fans down and he knew there would be lots of critics in the audience ready to pen their reviews. Certainly, he was feeling the pressure as he stepped onto the XL Center stage in Hartford, Connecticut.

He tweeted just before the show: 'Sorry been away all day...first tour ever. Little nervous. Don't want to let u guys down.'

Any nerves that he might have had didn't show in his performance, though: Justin put on an amazing show and the fans were blown away. He sounded even better live than he did on YouTube or on his albums. Afterwards he tweeted: '2nite was just... well...i was scared. didnt want to let anyone down but the energy and the fans were incredible. Cant wait to do this again!'

DID YOU KNOW?

For many of the dates, Justin's family – his mom, his grandparents, even his dog – were there with him. Once the tour moved outside of America and Canada, of course they couldn't attend every show, but Pattie still went to as many as possible. She will always be Justin's No. 1 fan!

One of Justin's most memorable performances was on 21 December 2011, when he performed at Massey Hall in Toronto. It's an iconic Canadian venue and so he decided to strip everything back and put on an acoustic show for his Canadian fans. Performing in Toronto was like coming home and he loved having lots of his family and friends in the audience. He felt really relaxed and asked the audience what songs they wanted him to sing rather than sticking to a set list. During the show, Justin's sister Jazmyn sang 'Baby' with him.

Justin tweeted afterwards: 'Tonight was special. No rules. Music, family, friends, fans, charity, and music. Thank you. #HomeForTheHolidays.'

DID YOU KNOW?

Justin loves sharing his new music with fans and, during one visit to Toronto in July 2013, he decided to give one group of Beliebers a special preview. The girls had been waiting for him outside his tour bus when he appeared and told them to turn off their mobiles. After they had done so, he played them some new tracks and sang 'Heartbreaker'. The girls couldn't believe what was happening and one tweeted Justin later to say: '@justinbieber HEARTBREAKER WAS AMAZING IT WAS SO GOOD THANK YOU FOR PLAYING IT FOR US.' They were definitely in the right place at the right time – what a privilege to hear Justin's music before anyone else!

When Justin and his crew were in Winnipeg in October 2012, they went out for some Japanese food and Justin had a go at cooking on a hibachi (a Japanese heating device). Dan Kanter posted a photo up and tweeted: 'Yup, doesn't just sing, dance, and play gtr, piano, and drums... He also cooks! #Hibachi in #Winnipeg.'

During Justin's performance of 'Beautiful' with Carly Rae Jepsen at the Credit Union Centre in Saskatoon on 16 October 2012, he nearly fell over. They were walking down some steps when Justin missed one and fell back two! Justin looked like he was going to topple over but thankfully Carly grabbed him and helped him steady himself.

When Justin was performing his Believe concert in Toronto on 1 December 2012, he had a special surprise for fans. Drake joined him onstage and, together, they sang their track 'Right Here'. The Beliebers watching loved it, as did Justin himself, as he tweeted afterwards: 'A night i will never forget. #TORONTO i love u. #HOME #CANADA thank u.'

To see a video of the performance, search on YouTube for 'Justin Bieber and Drake Toronto'. The show was also filmed for the 'Believe' 3D movie.

Justin has always been passionate about ice hockey and he was really touched when he was presented with a signed Toronto Maple Leafs hockey stick in a frame from the CEO of the team in July 2013. From an early age, he had always supported the Toronto

Maple Leafs. He used to love playing for his local team in Stratford and had wanted to be a professional player when he grew up. Also, he supported his local adult team 'the Cullitons' and would go to their matches with his grandpa.

Justin admits: 'I was never the kid that was, like, "Oh, I want to be famous". Or, "I want to be out there". I sang, but it was just for fun. I did a lot of different stuff. I played sports. Singing was just another hobby and I never took it seriously. I never got lessons.

'I use to practise my signature for hockey – it's kind of how I learned to give my autograph.'

DID YOU KNOW?

Justin has an Indian tattoo on his shoulder dedicated to his grandpa. It's the logo of the Stratford Cullitons. He posted up a photo of the tattoo on Instagram and explained: 'My grandfather always took me to the stratford culliton every friday night this is for u Grampa … My man @chenterios hooked it up.'

Canadian fans should check out the Justin Belieber Canada fan page on Facebook. Liked by over

202,000 Beliebers, it is run by superfan Steven. He says: 'im proud to be a belieber :) I haven't met justin bieber yet so my day will come :) Never Say Never, Right? so justin noticed me 3 times on twitter. he tweeted me on September 16, 2009 and Retweeted me on January 23, 2011 (: & tweeted my video I made for him on December 6th, 2011 !!!'

CODY'S STORY

Twenty-one-year-old Cody is from Toronto. His three favourite songs are 'Never Let You Go', 'Down To Earth' and 'Fall'. The things Cody likes most about Justin are: 'His music and what he does for his fans – not many artists are like that and, despite how big he is, he hasn't let fame get to him.

'Being from Canada, being a Belieber (or in my case as a *Boy* Belieber) is special as it's home for him. He's comfortable here so we give him that space and respect. I love taking part in fan events and I've taken photos and recorded the last three Toronto buy-outs. Whenever Justin releases an album everyone gets together, goes to the store, completely sells them out and donates the albums to a sick kids' hospital. To see one of my videos, just search for "Toronto Acoustic Believe Buy-out" on YouTube.

'The day I met Justin was 25 November 2012 – it was a VERY interesting day. With all the Grey Cup [the championship game of the Canadian Football League] festivities going on, it got very crazy but any fan of Justin's was either at the Rogers Centre for his half-time show performance OR at his hotel trying to meet him. For my friends and I, we decided to head to his hotel. We got there around 10am and there were already quite a few people there from the day before, where they had no luck at all. The weather was a tad bit cold but wasn't bad enough to make you have to leave.

'During the day his grandparents came out, said hi to us all and took pictures with fans. Justin's little sister Jazzy kept walking to the bus and back, and his little bro came to the door and waved to everyone. Dan [Kanter], Alfredo [Flores] and Scrappy [Stassen] came out and took a few photos before they went off to do their own thing, yet still no sight of Justin until 7pm, when he was leaving to go to the Grey Cup. He just walked by the door and waved. To say the least, a lot of us were upset but, on the other hand, it was a gamble to wait so we left to get something to eat, watch his performance, and after he was done we decided to go back and see if he would return.

'There was about ten of us waiting (but seemed like a lot more at the time). Fifteen minutes later Dan and Alfredo returned, but no sign of Justin until I poked my head around again to make sure and, at the same time, Justin was looking too and called us over for photos! It was a VERY quick process but he didn't even have to take pictures. His new bodyguard kept saying, "One more," but Justin didn't listen and was still telling fans to come over, which was really nice. For myself, this is a huge thing – I'll admit it, I wasn't a fan of him during "My World", I actually started being a fan after seeing him perform at the 2010 MMVAS and also hearing his song "Never Let You Go". It took me a while to actually tell people I'm a fan – well, 'cause I'm a twenty-one-year-old guy – but the friends I've made because of it is amazing. So here's what I say to anyone reading this, who hasn't met him yet: your time will come, and when it does the feelings you will have will be indescribable!'

LINDSAY'S STORY

Lindsay is fifteen and from Toronto. Her favourite three songs are 'She Don't Like The Lights', 'Runaway Love' and 'Bigger'. She says: 'What I love most about Justin is probably his smile, and how much he cares for all of his fans around the world. Being a Belieber in Canada is pretty cool, I guess since I'm from the same place as Justin. There's also a lot of Beliebers I've met the last few years and become friends with.

'My dream has always been to see Justin in concert, and well, it finally happened on 1 December 2012. It was Justin's concert here in Toronto. Sadly, my friends and I had no tickets. I woke up that day really early and headed out to the Rogers Centre with my friend to at least try and get a glimpse of Justin. We got to the venue and met up with the rest of our friends and the waiting began. Hours went by and we were waiting in the freezing cold. We walked around the Rogers Centre maybe a billion times.

'It was about four o'clock and all of the people with Meet & Greets started heading in. Five guys and two cameramen came outside and a lady followed behind with a sign saying, "BELIEVE MOVIE BEING FILMED". We all went crazy, everyone started singing; it was an amazing feeling being with Beliebers, singing to Justin's songs and being filmed for the movie. After the camera crew left, we were waiting in front of a door and we saw [film director] Jon Chu. He waved at us, said hi and left. The concert was going to start in a bit and we started losing hope. We thought we were never going to see Justin, Scooter [Braun] or anyone.

'We wanted to get into the concert so bad. We started talking to people who worked at the venue – people who put the stage together, Justin's crew, basically anyone. The concert had started and we were all depressed, except for one of my friends who said, "Justin told us to never say never." She kept us waiting in the cold longer. Then, as eight o'clock came around, we were going to leave; it was too cold to stand around anymore. As we were walking to leave, we saw a man with a camera filming one of Justin's dancers and Scooter. We all ran to him, crying, telling him how long we had been waiting outside, etc. He said he had no tickets but he'd take a picture with us. The six of us lined up to take a picture with him but then he said, "I only have five tickets, one of you can't come in." My heart broke – all that waiting and one of us, sadly, couldn't go. My friend said it was okay; she wouldn't come with us. But then Scooter said to her, "You can't sit with them, but you're coming to watch the show with me." WE ALL WENT CRAZY! We started crying, screaming; my friend even looked like she was going to pass out. He gave us front-row tickets. I hugged him and we ran in so fast, screaming and crying. People were looking at us weird. We got into the venue and into our seats about ten minutes before Justin came out. When Justin came out, everyone went WILD!

'After the concert, I went home and went straight to bed. I woke up the next morning with a tweet from Scooter and a follow from him. It was the best day of my life and I owe it all to Scooter Braun. I will never be able to thank him enough for what he did for us that day.'

CHAPTER 9

CHINA

When Justin arrived in China on his My World Tour, he was greeted by only seven Beliebers, which the media claimed proved that he wasn't very popular. They couldn't have been more wrong as there are lots of Beliebers in China, but because Justin arrived during school time his fans were in class: truancy is taken very seriously there.

Justin performed in Chek Lap Kok at the AsiaWorld Arena on 13 May 2011 in front of nearly 14,000 fans. He had some days off, so was able to explore Hong Kong too. He was amazed at all the different foods and gadgets on sale – it was so different to anywhere else he had visited.

Sadly, Justin didn't get the chance to visit China as

part of his Believe Tour in 2012/2013, which was disappointing for his Chinese fans. Superfan Lisa Chan decided to make a special video for Justin, which she posted on YouTube. In it she says: 'Hey, Justin Bieber and all the fans who love JB, this is Lisa Chan. Me and some JB China fans made this video to show Justin Bieber how much we love him!!!!'

In the video, Lisa shows different Chinese fans with Justin's albums and photos, and their individual messages to Justin. They all want Justin to visit China again.

DID YOU KNOW?

While he was in China, Justin hired a yacht for the day. He had great fun on the water with his crew and mom Pattie.

Chinese fans created an event called 'Searching For Justin Bieber', which was a unique way of showing Justin how much he means to them. They collected photographs of the words 'Justin Bieber' spelled out on sand, on condensation, using beads, Rubik's Cubes and in many different ways; they even found JB number plates and created pieces of art for the project. The best images were included in a special video set to a beautiful piece of music, just for Justin.

CHAPTER 10

DENMARK

Justin performed his My World concert in Denmark on 1 April 2011. For an April Fools' joke, he got Kenny Hamilton to sing 'Baby', which was really funny. During the trip, Justin and his crew stayed in a very unusual hotel in the middle of nowhere. The hotel used to be a lunatic asylum before it was converted into a hotel and it freaked Justin out a bit.

While in the country, Justin met World Heavyweight boxing champion Evander Holyfield, who was in Copenhagen to watch a big fight. The two stars had their photo taken together, and the boxer signed some gloves and a skateboard for Justin. He might have been star-struck but Evander was equally so: he couldn't wait to tell his kids he had met Justin.

Just over a month later, on 7 May 2011, 400 Danish Beliebers decided to hold a Bieber Parade in Copenhagen. Superfan Emma Lund made a video of the event, with help from Lisa Kastleen and Jannie Buhl (the girls run the 'Justin Bieber Danmark' Facebook page, which has over 100,000 fans). The fans sang some of Justin's songs, danced and celebrated being Beliebers together. There were quite a few boy Beliebers at the event and fans had made some fantastic banners, asking Justin to come back to Denmark. The event was such a success that the girls arranged another Bieber Parade for July 2011.

Justin visited Denmark in June 2012 to promote his *Believe* album. So many fans turned up at the location of the press conference that the whole building had to be evacuated for safety reasons. There were hundreds of fans chanting outside, desperate to catch a glimpse of Justin. Thankfully, some journalists and presenters still managed to talk with him individually.

Morten Resen, the presenter of the TV series *Go'Morgen Danmark*, enjoyed meeting Justin and asked what being a Christian and believing in God means to him. Justin replied: 'I think it's just important; it's something that keeps me grounded. I talk to Him. I wouldn't be in this position without God so I make sure to honour Him.'

Justin always says that he is grateful to God for

everything He has done for him, and will always remember this when he prays.

Much to the delight of Justin's many Danish Beliebers, he performed his Believe concert on 20 April 2013 at the Parken Stadium in Copenhagen. Before the show, when Justin was doing Meet & Greets, fans noticed that he had a new tattoo of a koi carp on his arm.

DID YOU KNOW?

Justin loves playing hide and seek with his crew – he's really good at it. He also likes playing video games such as Mario Kart and NBA 2K.

VERONICA'S STORY

Seventeen-year-old Veronica is from Copenhagen. Her favourite songs are 'Out Of Town Girl', 'Take You' and 'Beauty And A Beat'. Veronica sometimes finds being a Belieber in Denmark annoying. She explains: 'I live far away from Justin, his whole crew. Everything, like his perfumes, magazines about him, etc., always comes out first in America and I feel I have to wait like 39583495 years, or another huge number, before I can buy it in my country, if at all. Justin always tweets when I am asleep – I hate that! Time zones are a right pain; I love being a Belieber, though.

'I love taking part in fan events and flash mobs. Two girls in my country called Jannie and Lisa have organised a lot of flash mobs, Bieber Parades and events since 2009. I have been to many of them and I love it! I meet so many sweet Beliebers and friends I have made through Facebook and Twitter. Spending time with Beliebers at a Bieber Parade or a flash mob is great!'

DID YOU KNOW?

Justin thinks giving money to charity is so important and because of this he makes sure that for every concert ticket, bottle of perfume or piece of merchandise sold a proportion goes to his charity, Pencils of Promise, or to the Make-A-Wish Foundation.

Veronica met Justin in April 2013. She says: 'Me and six other girls found out that Justin was staying at the Bella Sky Comwell Hotel in Copenhagen and decided to go there; all the other Beliebers were at the wrong hotel. We were quiet because we know how annoying it can be when people scream loud, especially for

Justin. It was cold and windy that day. Two of the girls had to pee and asked a security guard from the hotel if they could use the hotel's toilet. The security guard said yes and we saw the girls go into the hotel. Right after they came out, they smiled so big and said, "Girls, we need to be quiet, but listen, Scooter Braun is in the building! He is in the lobby with his computer." Seconds later, who should walk out but Scooter! He was in a rush because he had to catch a flight, but he let us have a photo with him. After he left, we all hugged and screamed so loud. He helped Justin become the worldwide famous artist he is today!

'When I was on my way home I checked my emails on my phone. There was one new message: I had won a Meet & Greet with Justin the next day! I couldn't believe it – I was going to meet Justin with my friend Boutayna. The next day at around 4pm, we got in line for the Meet & Greet and went into a room. While we were waiting, we saw Dan Kanter. Suddenly they start letting people in. The line was moving and I was getting closer and closer to Justin. People who had gotten their picture had to walk up some stairs and I saw a lot of them crying. I looked at my friend and said, "I can't hold back my tears anymore!" She looked at me and said, "Veronica, please don't! You don't want to look like an idiot next to Justin, right?" She was right.

'Now it was my turn. I went into the room and the first person I saw was [Justin's friend] Lil Za (he is so cute, by the way). Then I looked to the left and I saw him. He was standing right there, my lifesaver – the person I have seen on pictures and videos and now he was in front of me in real life: Justin Drew Bieber. The time stopped for, like, three seconds. I looked at his face – he looked like a doll, a wax figure or something. I couldn't believe my own eyes. He looked even better in real life. Justin suddenly looked at ME! He smiled and he said, "Heeeyy!" He indicated that I should come over on his right side and stand by him. He put his arms around me and I put my arms around his waist. I could feel his back; he was so soft. We looked into the camera and it went so quickly, and suddenly we were out of the room; I started crying.

'I can finally say that I have met Justin – Justin Bieber. I had been waiting to meet him for so long.'

EMMA'S STORY

Seventeen-year-old Emma is from Copenhagen. Her favourite three songs are 'Believe', 'Never Say Never' and 'Love Me'. She has been a Belieber since 2009, and in May 2012 was due to meet Justin in Oslo, but the event was cancelled for security reasons. Emma was devastated and cried for five hours. She finally met him on 20 April 2013 and it was well worth the wait. Emma says: 'He is such a loving and caring person. He's truly amazing! He is so thankful to every fan who supports him. It felt amazing, finally meeting him in person – it was like being in a dream.'

CHRISTINA'S STORY

Christina is sixteen and from Klim. Her favourite songs are 'Down To Earth' ('because it's a very emotional song'), 'Pray' ('because it has a beautiful message') and 'Believe' ('because Justin was this little boy who just had a dream, and that dream came true because he believed and worked hard').

Christina takes part in fan events through the internet. When she met Justin at Denmark's national stadium in Copenhagen on 20 April 2013, it was a dream come true. She explains: 'I remember being just a little kid, watching this amazing boy on YouTube, and I couldn't even understand English at that time. Justin has taught me so much! I fell in love with him immediately – his personality, his hair, his humour, his amazing charisma... yeah, everything about him. I love what he stands for: to BELIEVE. I've always been one of these girls who had never believed in herself. Sometimes I would actually cry because everything felt hopeless, like I had no future. I feel like I know Justin, and to know that he didn't even know I existed made me so depressed. But boys and girls, dreams DO come true! I'm from the little country of Denmark and I've been that person who could only dream about meeting Justin. The world seemed too damn big, and I would never meet him. On April 20th, my dream came true on the "Believe" Tour.

'I was one of the lucky people who got a VIP ticket, out of 45,000 people! I can't describe how lucky I felt, it was surreal. My parents were really sweet to drive me five hours to see his concert, since we live far from Copenhagen. We arrived at "Parken" (where the concert took place) at 9am and we had to wait for eight hours before we were let in.

'All of us who had VIP tickets were let into a big room, where we got a lot of information. We were all really excited and time went by fast. Suddenly there were only about five minutes before we got to meet Justin. While we were standing there, I was thinking how long have I been waiting for this moment? I couldn't believe it! I was led to a black curtain. One of Justin's bodyguards stood there and he asked me, "Are you ready?" I said, "I think so," and then he said, "Take a deep breath," and he pulled the black curtain to the side. There Justin stood, so perfect – he was so cute and so grown up. I went over to him and gave him a quick hug before we took a picture. It was so surreal, like I was flying, and watched my body standing beside Justin's. We had no time with him (which was sad), but it was still amazing, a dream come true. And the concert – it was beyond words!'

LAURA'S STORY

Seventeen-year-old Laura is from Aabenraa. Her favourite three songs are 'One Less Lonely Girl', 'Fall' and 'Be Alright'. Laura likes having friends who like Justin because they can talk about him together. She wishes people wouldn't say nasty things about Justin and that they would at least respect him and what he has achieved. Laura has taken part in two flash mobs: the first one was just before his first concert in Denmark on 1 April 2011 and the second flash mob was on 20 April 2013 before his second concert. She would love to take part in a Bieber Parade, but they have never been close enough for her to attend.

Laura met Justin on 2 April 2013 in Hamburg. She says: 'I was so nervous and couldn't believe my own eyes. Justin was right in front of me! All I could think was, "Is this a dream?!?!" It was so unbelievable. I refused to believe that this was actually happening. I was standing next to JUSTIN BIEBER! I put my arm around him, and my other hand on his six-pack. I could feel his abs through his tank top – it was amazing! I told him I loved him and stuff. He said, "Thank you, sweetie," with his cute accent and a big smile on his face.

'I met him – it may have been only for a couple of seconds but it was the best seconds of my entire life! He was absolutely perfect.'

CHAPTER 11

DOMINICAN REPUBLIC

Four American Beliebers filmed a very cute video while they were doing charity work in the Dominican Republic, showing children performing Justin's hit 'Baby'. They posted it on YouTube and sent it to the Justin Bieber fan site *JustinBieberZone.com* in August 2011. To see the video, search for 'Lecheria sings Baby'.

In their accompanying message they wrote: 'We are 4 American volunteers working in a poor Haitian community outside of Santo Domingo, Dominican Republic. After introducing our students to Justin Bieber, we found that they immediately LOVED his music, even though they don't speak English. These children don't have much in their lives and we wanted to do something fun and exciting for them. So, when hearing that Justin Bieber was coming to Santo Domingo for a concert, we decided to make a video of our students singing and dancing to BABY.

'Unfortunately, Justin cancelled this concert to the DR, but we decided to go ahead with the video. The kids were having so much fun with it, really trying to learn the lyrics. They were always asking us to translate what Justin was saying so they could understand. After a while, it was pretty commonplace to be walking around the community and hear a child singing "Baby".

'Originally we thought Justin was coming to Santo Domingo in April so we thought we could catch his eye with this video. That concert was cancelled but we decided to go ahead with the filming.

'JUSTIN COME VISIT US!!!'

Volunteer Sarah and her friends got their wish in October 2013, when Justin performed his Believe concert in Santo Domingo, but before then he popped over for a holiday. In June 2013, Justin stayed at the Casa de Campo Golf Resort. He had been so busy touring Europe, Asia and Africa that he needed a break before his North American dates.

The Casa de Campo Golf Resort has three golf courses: the Teeth of the Dog course is the best golf course in the Caribbean, and the Dye Fore and the

Links courses are pretty special too. Some of the best golfers in the world have stayed at the Casa de Campo Golf Resort and it is very expensive. Justin and his friends stayed in a villa previously used by Jay-Z and Beyoncé when Jay-Z was celebrating his birthday in December 2009.

During his holiday, a photo of Justin standing by a pool was circulated on the internet, with fans wondering who the woman who took the photo was, as her legs are visible in the shot. A local website called Casa de Campo Living didn't reveal who the mystery woman was, but said that Justin was staying with approximately thirteen other people, including Jaden Smith (son of actors Will Smith and Jada Pinkett Smith) and T Jr. (son of *The A Team* actor Mr. T).

DID YOU KNOW?

One day, Justin will be going into space! Sir Richard Branson tweeted on 6 June 2013: 'Great to hear @justinbieber & @scooterbraun are latest @virgingalactic future astronauts. Congrats, see you up there!

'@justinbieber @scooterbraun @virgingalactic music video in space? Now that's what I call music!'

But Justin and Scooter aren't the only future space tourists: Hollywood actors Leonardo DiCaprio and Ashton Kutcher have also signed up but they will have to wait a while as it may be a few years before the programme starts.

Justin had tweeted in March 2013: 'I wanna do a concert in space' – maybe he will end up getting his wish.

KARLA'S STORY

Fifteen-year-old Karla is from Santo Domingo. She has been a Belieber since December 2009. Her favourite three songs are 'Down To Earth', 'Fall' and 'First Dance'. She says: 'Being a Belieber in the Dominican Republic is hard in some ways because Justin doesn't visit often, in fact his first show was on 22 October 2013. However, there are lots of Beliebers here and we have reunions and meetings.'

Karla went all the way to New York to see Justin with her friend and her aunt. They waited outside the NBC Studios because Justin was performing on *The Today Show* but, sadly, just missed him. Karla did get to see Justin's dancers, Dan Kanter (who said goodbye to her) and DJ James, though. They hung around for a couple more hours and saw Kenny Hamilton and

Alfredo Flores. Karla managed to hug them and got two photos taken with Kenny. She takes up the story: 'They're truly amazing – Alfredo is so nice and cute, I have a crush on him – and Kenny is so adorable.

'We found out that Justin was doing a signing at the J&R store so we got two wristbands so we could meet him on June 19th. When the day came we couldn't get over how long the line of fans was, but the line moved fast and before long we were near the front. Ryan came out and held my hand. When I saw Justin, I started shaking. I saw Alfredo and he winked at me, and I couldn't take it all in. Kenny said: "Nice to see you guys again" and I was so shocked because he remembered us, so I just replied, "Hola, Kenny." Justin was by his side and I gave him my *Believe* CD to sign. He is so perfect. I asked him if he could hold my hand and he said, "Sure" and took my hand.'

Later on, Karla went to MTV in Times Square because Justin was due there at 7pm and she waited outside for him with her aunt and friend. At 9pm, she saw his car leave and followed it, making her way back to the Eventi hotel, where Justin and his crew were staying. She went back to the hotel in the days that followed, and on 22 June she saw Scooter Braun. On other visits, she met Christian, Caitlin B and Jasmine.

Karla has had lots of success on Twitter: she tweeted Alfredo on 3 August 2012 and got a reply;

Justin retweeted one of her messages on 1 December 2012 and this made her cry tears of happiness. Alfredo also tweeted her on her birthday and Justin retweeted another of her messages. She would encourage all fans to try tweeting Justin and his crew because 'You never know, you might get a reply back.'

CHAPTER 12

FINLAND

Justin didn't visit Finland with his My World Tour but he did perform his Believe Tour in Helsinki on 26 April 2013. When his *Believe* album was released, he held a special release/listening party for Finnish Beliebers on 19 June 2012. Sadly, he couldn't make it in person but he did record a special message for fans, which was projected onto a big screen. In his message, he said: 'What's up, Finland? I just want to say thank you for all your support and I hope you enjoy my new album, *Believe*. Swaggy!'

If you are a Finnish Belieber, you should become a fan of the 'Justin Bieber Finland' community on Facebook.

SINI'S STORY

Sini is fifteen and from Helsinki, the capital of Finland. Her favourite three songs are 'I Would', 'Believe' and 'One Time'. She says: 'Being a Belieber in Finland is kind of lonely. There're not many big fan events or anything like that and I don't know many people who actually like Justin's music.'

She takes up her story: 'It all started when the "Believe" Tour dates were announced. I was sad to find out there [were] no tour dates in Finland but there was a tour date in Stockholm, Sweden, so I begged my mom to buy me tickets; she did. We got floor tickets and I was so freaking excited – I was gonna see my idol! Then one morning I was lying in my bed when I got a phone call from a Belieber friend of mine that I got to know through Twitter. She told me Justin was coming to Finland. I couldn't believe it, my idol was coming to my country!

'When the phone call ended, I googled it and it was true! The concert was gonna be the smallest one in the whole tour, there [were] only going to be about 12,000 people there. We decided to ask our parents for Meet & Greet tickets and her [my friend's] parents agreed but my parents were hesitant. The tickets cost a whole lot of money but I told them I would pay for at least half of them and sell the tickets we had originally bought for Sweden. Thankfully, they agreed.

'Nine months later, on 25 April, the day before the concert, I went in front of Justin's hotel. The hotel was called Kämp and it's located in Helsinki. I saw some of his dancers and his bodyguard. Then things started to get a bit crazy so I left. It was Justin's day off and I felt like I was disturbing his peace.

'On the day of the concert I had an entrance exam at a high school and, after that, we headed straight to the Hartwall Arena in Helsinki. It was raining so my hair got messed up, but I really didn't mind. Justin was two hours late so we missed the opening act but we didn't mind. Eventually Justin showed up and the Meet & Greets started. We all got in line. The first thing I saw of Justin was his quiff. I saw him a few times while standing in the line but I didn't freak out or anything like that – he's not a God, just a human like all of us. I left two of my drawings on a table we were told to put our gifts on; I doubt he got them, though.

'When I walked into the Meet & Greet area, he looked straight into my eyes and I said "Hi." I can still see his eyes now when I think about it. I stood next to him and we took the picture, and I got pushed away. It was really quick but I was happy.

'I walked into the arena and it was full of screaming Beliebers. We walked to the front of the floor. There was an area for us right in front of the stage. The concert was an amazing experience. I was so happy to see the person whose songs I'd been listening to for years performing them live right in front of me. To me, seeing him perform was more important than meeting him. I had promised myself not to take many pictures or videos (I ended up with nine pictures and one video). I just wanted to enjoy the concert live, not through videos. I also promised not to cry – I ended up tearing up during "Believe", though. I was holding up a sign that said "WE BELIEVE" and Justin looked at it and then at me. The whole experience was amazing – the concert was better than I could have ever imagined.'

There's nothing Justin loves more than saying hello to his fans. He finds time to take a selfie with a Belieber while performing on the *Today Show*, and high-fives fans on the way up to receive an award at the MuchMusic Video Awards in his home country, Canada.

© *Press Association Images*

Ilenia and Lizzy took some amazing photos of Justin while they were watching him live in concert. You can see just how big the crowds are at his performances, and how much passion he puts into each and every show.

Above: Justin gives so much of his time and money to charity and, when he heard about the devastating typhoon in the Philippines, he immediately started a campaign to raise money to help the survivors.

Below: While he was visiting the Philippines Justin raised spirits by playing a game of basketball with the children he met, and he later held a special signing session for them. He knows he is very fortunate to be so successful, and he always wants to help people who are suffering in any way he can.

Above left: There are many ways to meet Justin Bieber, whether at signings or Meet and Greets. You should never give up your dreams of meeting him.

Above right and below: Wherever he is, Justin always makes time to take pictures with his Beliebers. He knows how much it means to them, and loves making his fans happy.

© *Press Association Images*

Above: The only thing better than a Justin Bieber concert is to be privately serenaded by Justin himself. A few lucky girls were chosen for this experience as One Less Lonely Girls.

© *Rex Features*

Below: Holly managed her dream of meeting Justin and has the photographs to remind herself of how happy she was at that moment. Holly was also lucky enough to have her book signed as well.

Left: Justin Bieber has fans all over the world and, when he does world tours, crowds welcome him wherever he goes.

Right: Beliebers everywhere show support for Justin in any way they can, just like this young Belgian fan.

Left: A group of Mexican fans show their excitement and show off their posters before a gig in Mexico City.

© *Press Association Images*

Left: Thousands of fans caused chaos (in a good way) when Justin Bieber arrived for a concert in Norway.

Right: The superstar himself, looking great in all-white, in full flow performing in the USA.

Below: When Justin Bieber did a rare open-air concert in Germany, thousands of Beliebers flocked to see him, all of them wanting a picture as a memento of their great day.

© *Press Association Images*

So many people have had their dreams come true and met their hero – Never Say Never, the next time it could be you. (*Clockwise from above left*) Anna from Austria was stunned to be chosen as Justin's One Less Lonely Girl. Gaia from Italy was able to interview Justin – and she got a hug! Tara from London thought she had missed her chance to meet Justin, but she was so happy when she finally did. Belgian Klara was able to meet Justin backstage briefly. Kim from Holland travelled all the way to New York to meet Justin. Australian Sophie also travelled to New York to see Justin, and made two lucky Beliebers' day when she gave away two Meet and Greet tickets!

CHAPTER 13

FRANCE

Justin loves visiting France – he adores the culture and meeting French Beliebers. He has visited the country many times. He performed in France on 29 March 2011 as part of his My World Tour and then performed his Believe concert there on 19 March and 8 April 2013. When Justin visited Paris, he took time out to visit the Louvre Museum, which is where the famous painting the *Mona Lisa* is on display. Once surrounded by fans he had to leave though, because he didn't want to disrupt the other visitors, who were trying to enjoy the exhibitions.

When Justin was in Paris, promoting his *My World 2.0* album, he performed at the Eiffel Tower on 24 February 2010. This was a big deal as not many artists have been given the opportunity to sing from the world-famous landmark.

DID YOU KNOW?

Justin held a premiere for his movie *Never Say Never* in Paris on 17 February 2011.

On 30 January 2012, Justin went to the NRJ Music Awards in Cannes, where he picked up the Award of Honor. He was really touched and tweeted: 'i never thought i would ever get out of stratford and now im celebrating in france. never gets old. ALWAYS grateful! #Ilovemyfans ... Je t'aime BELIEBERS!'

In 2011, he had won the International Revelation of the Year award but had been unable to attend the award ceremony owing to his busy schedule.

Some fans waited for him at Nice Airport to say goodbye but Justin couldn't stop. He used Twitter to explain what happened and to apologise to fans, tweeting: 'the other day in the airport i got surrounded by 20 paps. I dont like small spaces and i just wanted to get on the plane. I ran to get thru the gate and there is a video of me running by fans and on the other side you dont see the 20 paps. I would never run by my fans...

'and for those that i did pass that day I AM SORRY.

I know my fans are my everything. I know my responsibility to them. I LOVE MY BELIEBERS.

'so as i get older i know i will learn to deal with these things better and better just still learning. still human. just had to get that out.'

Justin visited France again in May 2012 to promote his album *Believe* in Paris. On 31 May, he injured himself by walking into a glass wall while performing a special show for Beliebers. He told *TMZ*: 'I was performing, and I was going offstage and basically, I'm in Paris and performing on the tallest building in Paris, and there's a glass wall behind me, but there's a railing behind the glass. And so I went to reach for the railing and I hit my head on the glass. And I guess me and glass windows don't really go together.'

Poor Justin ended up getting concussion and passing out for fifteen seconds once he had walked offstage. He tweeted fans later on to update them on how he was feeling:

'Thanks for the love but there are alot of people out there who need prayers. im fine. just smacked my head and needed some water. all good. im Canadian. we are tough. lol. its all good. just gotta take it easy the rest of the night. back at it again for u guys tomorrow. Thanks.

'The fact you all knew what happened before my mom even did is impressive. lol. I have amazing fans. very grateful for your love.

'Gonna eat, rest, get some sleep and tomorrow Im back at it. The show must go on! Love yall. We got this.'

The next day, Justin decided to do a sing-a-long with Dan Kanter and hundreds of fans from the balcony of Universal Music's offices. Before arriving at the venue he tweeted: 'about to head over to 20-22, rue des Fossés Saint-Jacques here in PARIS! who is coming to sing with me and #WithDanKanter.'

Hundreds of fans turned up, so Justin had to use a megaphone to be heard over their screams. He and his French Beliebers sang 'Baby' and 'Boyfriend', with Dan playing acoustic guitar. For the fans in attendance, it was an amazing experience.

Sometimes Justin has to change hotels for safety reasons, and this happened during his stay in Paris. On 18 March 2013, he had to move from the Hotel Le Meurice to the Mandarin Oriental. Five hundred fans had turned up at the Hotel Le Meurice and, because the hotel didn't have an underground entrance and garage he could use, it was thought that it would be best if he moved to another hotel.

During his Believe concert at the Zénith de

Strasbourg arena in April 2013, fans held up 'Forever Belieber' signs to show Justin how much he means to them. To see a video, search on YouTube for 'Justin Bieber Believe Tour Strasbourg'.

Cody Simpson really enjoyed being Justin's support act in France and throughout Europe. He had never visited Europe before the Believe Tour and enjoyed checking out the Eiffel Tower at one o'clock in the morning with Justin (they decided to go at that time because it meant they could walk around undisturbed). Cody's performance at the Palais Omnisport de Paris Bercy arena was his last show of the tour so Justin went onstage and gave him a big hug.

Justin and Cody weren't the only ones to love Paris. Justin's mom Pattie tweeted: 'Loved spending time w my baby @justinbieber & nana & papa today in Paris. #beautiful.'

DID YOU KNOW?

During their stay in Paris, Justin and his dancers visited the famous Moulin Rouge. Justin has so many dedicated French Beliebers, the Justin Bieber France Facebook page has over 1.2 million fans!

ROXANNE'S STORY

Eighteen-year-old Roxanne is from Grenoble. Her favourite three songs are 'Be Alright', 'Fall' and 'One Time'. Roxanne likes organising Justin Bieber fan meetings for French fans. She has been a Belieber for five years, but 2013 was by far her favourite year as she explains: 'I went to the "Believe" Tour in London on 8 March, and I slept in the same hotel as Justin! That was CRAZY! I saw all of the Bieber team and I even got a hug from Alfredo [Flores]. I also saw Chaz [Somers] and he said "Hi" to me. I went to the "Believe" Tour in Paris on 19 March, and the show was perfect! Then I went to the "Believe" Tour in Strasbourg on 8 April with a friend to the Meet & Greet. A nice guy gave us the key from the "Believe" Tour!

'Meeting Justin was the best moment of my life. When I saw him, I had a huge smile on my face and Justin smiled too. We took the picture and Justin said, "Thank you" and he caressed my back – I was the happiest girl in the world. After the Meet & Greet we returned backstage and we saw Justin on his Segway with a mask on. He laughed; it was really cute. Afterwards we went into the pit and saw the show. Dan [Kanter] gave me some guitar picks, which I will always treasure as a memento of the day I met Justin.'

CHAPTER 14

GERMANY

Justin performed his My World Tour concert on 26 March 2011 in Oberhausen and on 2 April in Berlin. He also performed 'Pray' and 'Never Say Never' on the *Wetten, dass..?* TV show. Justin performed his Believe Tour concert on 28 March 2013 in Munich, on 31 March in Berlin, on 2 April in Hamburg, on 3 April in Frankfurt, on 5 April in Dortmund and on 6 April in Cologne.

When it was Pattie's birthday, Justin was performing his My World Tour show in Berlin, and he wanted all the Beliebers watching his show to see how much his mom means to him. He presented her with a lovely cake and she was overwhelmed. When she went to blow out the candles, her hair caught fire but

Justin quickly put it out! That night he also gave her a copy of him singing the Boyz II Men track 'Mama' – she loved it.

DID YOU KNOW?

Justin took his family with him when he visited Germany in June 2012. He performed 'Boyfriend' on the final of *Germany's Next Top Model* TV show, starring German model and TV host Heidi Klum.

In September 2012, Justin visited Germany again to promote his book *Justin Bieber: Just Getting Started* and album *Believe*. Before he arrived, he tweeted a photo of himself on Instagram with the message: 'Airport. On da way to Germany

'EUROPE here we come! #JustGettingStarted.'

During the promotional trip, Justin was interviewed by Reuters TV and he chatted about his albums, saying: 'I think my musical development is going to change throughout my whole career. I think that each album is going to be different, and something new that the fans will never expect because, if I do the same thing every album, I don't want my fans to get bored.'

On 11 September, he performed a special intimate show for 500 of his biggest German Beliebers in Frankfurt. The event was completely free and he performed an acoustic version of 'As Long As You Love Me' with Dan Kanter on guitar. The fans felt very privileged to see Justin up close and personal. This wasn't the first time he had played an intimate show in Germany; in June 2012, he had performed 'Die In Your Arms' for sixty fans in Berlin.

When Justin visited Germany in 2013, Adidas NEO decided to hold a special party in their Hamburg store. They had Justin's DJ, DJ Tay James, provide the music and as well as Justin, of course, they invited some of Germany's most dedicated Beliebers. Fans had their nails painted while they waited and then spent time with Justin getting their photos taken.

DID YOU KNOW?

Justin's favourite songs to perform live are 'Out Of Town Girl', 'Catching Feelings' and 'Take You'.

After landing in Munich in March 2013, Justin's pet monkey Mally was seized by German customs because he didn't have the right paperwork (he had been given Mally as a nineteenth birthday present by a music producer). Mally is a capuchin monkey and animal rights campaigners wanted Justin to give him up permanently so he could live with other monkeys rather than with Justin and his crew. In April 2013, the media reported that Justin had done just that and Mally was to have a new home with members of his own species.

If you are a German Belieber, you should become a fan of 'Justin Bieber Germany' on Facebook. The fan page has over 45,000 likes.

SOPHIA'S STORY

Sophia is fifteen and from Stuttgart. Her favourite three songs are 'Be Alright', 'Down To Earth' and 'Believe'. The things she loves most about Justin are 'how he treats his fans, his personality and of course his music'. She thinks being a German Belieber is great and she has found lots of friendly fans through Justin. Sophia takes part in Justin events all the time as there is a Belieber meeting every month in Stuttgart: fans get together and sing some of Justin's songs.

After winning a competition, Sophia met Justin on 28 March 2013 in Munich. She also saw Kenny Hamilton and, although the meeting with them was short, she will never forget it. She says: 'I had an amazing time and I still can't believe that I met my idol after more than three years of waiting. I know sometimes it's really hard to believe in "Never Say Never" and "Believe", but please don't give up! Every true Belieber is going to meet Justin one day, sooner or later your time will come!'

CHAPTER 15

IRELAND

Justin performed his My World Tour concert in Ireland on 8 March 2011. Two years later, he performed his Believe Tour concert there on 17 and 18 February 2013, supported by Cody Simpson.

Before Justin arrived in Ireland in February 2013 to perform his Believe show at the O2 Arena in Dublin, he took some time off to relax. He tweeted: 'next time i hit the stage will be in Dublin but until then Im gonna take a little time for me. #familytime

'2 more days and the #BELIEVEtour starts back up in EUROPE in DUBLIN! u guys ready. Im chillin on this beach until then.'

Even though he was on holiday, he still filmed a video for fans to show them some new music, and had his brother and sister come and say 'hi'. Justin is always thinking of Beliebers and apologised for having slow internet as it was stopping him from going on Ustream.

Once he was in Ireland, he filmed a short video clip of himself ripping off Alfredo's sleeves with his bare hands. He also tweeted: 'Two years later WE ARE BACK!! Same hotel, Same spot, ripping more sleeves. Love you bro @alfredoflores! Miss you @OfficialJaden.'

After his performance at the O2 Arena in Dublin, he went clubbing at Everleigh Garden.

DID YOU KNOW?

Justin has befriended Niall Horan from One Direction, who is from Ireland. When Justin was performing in Dublin, some of Niall's best friends from home went to see the show.

Irish Beliebers really want Justin to visit their country more often but they understand that he is a worldwide artist so has so many different countries to visit. They want to try to get him to notice them more so they have set up a Facebook page called 'Bring Justin Bieber to Ireland!' If you are an Irish

Belieber, why not become a fan of the page today and join the campaign?

On 22 March 2013, superfan Gabrielle Kavanagh asked fans to help get #JustinWatchProjectShamrockVIDEO trending on Twitter at 7pm because she wanted Justin to see a special video she had made with other Irish Beliebers. To see the video for yourself, search on YouTube for #ProjectShamrock Dublin, Believe Tour 2013. The video starts with the message: 'When we found out Justin Bieber was coming back to Ireland for his "Believe" Tour, us Irish Beliebers were so happy! Justin doesn't come here that much so we wanted to do something so he would remember his Irish Beliebers! So @xrroisonx (Roisin) came up with an amazing idea! # ProjectShamrock!'

Roisin's idea was to make shamrocks out of card that Beliebers could hold up when Justin sang 'Believe' during his Irish concerts. This would leave a lasting impression on him and would be a nice memento for Irish Beliebers to keep. To help spread the word, Roisin and her friends set up Project Shamrock Facebook and Twitter accounts and encouraged fans to make as many shamrocks as they could to hand out to other Beliebers once they arrived at the O2 Arena.

The girls certainly got their wish: Justin noticed the

shamrocks and #ProjectShamrock trended on Twitter. In a message on their video, they wrote: 'So Justin might not have tweeted about #ProjectShamrock but Pattie tweeted a picture of it on her Instagram and one of Justin's dancers held up a Belieber's shamrock during "Believe".'

Fellow Irish Beliebers loved the project, which brought all Irish Beliebers together. Huge Justin fan Chloe McGuiness from Dundalk was really impressed and tweeted: 'I really love the #projectshamrock idea ☺ whoever came up with it is a genius.'

DID YOU KNOW?

When Justin's dancer Nick DeMoura tweeted, 'Ireland you were great! #believetour' Justin replied, 'better than great.'

CHAPTER 16

ISRAEL

During his World Tour, Justin performed in Tel Aviv, Israel, on 14 April 2011. The media reported that he was paid $1 million for the show in front of 20,000 fans at Hayarkon Park, but that promoters had been hoping 35,000 Beliebers would have seen the show. No official word came from Justin's team, but 20,000 fans is still a huge amount.

While in Israel, he enjoyed a week's holiday with his family and Scooter Braun so they could visit Jerusalem. It meant so much to Justin to be walking where Jesus walked and visiting places he had read about in the Bible. However, during his stay, he found the Israeli paparazzi very intrusive and tweeted: 'i want to see this country and all the places i've dreamed of and whether its the paps or being pulled into politics its been frustrating.'

Justin told Channel 10: 'I love my fans here in Israel, I really support them; they've been amazing to me so I'm really glad to be here, it's beautiful. I'm going to go have some fun.'

DID YOU KNOW?

Justin went indoor snowboarding and had fun in a dune buggy during his time in Israel.

During an interview with an Israeli news channel, Scooter Braun was asked how he came to manage Justin. He explained: 'Justin's mother is a devout Christian and she at first didn't really want him going into the music business at all and, if he was, she wanted him singing Christian music. Justin wanted to do pop and R&B, and I think when she thought she was going to find a manager for him, if she was going to do it, she thought it would be a Christian man and she prayed on it and she feels that God told her to go with me, a Jew.'

He also revealed that they pray together before each show. Scooter explained: 'We do a prayer, every show; we all get in a huddle and Justin and the crew say a prayer in the name of Jesus, Amen and then myself and Dan, our musical director, we're Jews so we would always say the Shema [the central prayer in the Jewish prayer book]. And Justin's a sponge, he picks things up, so it was like the fourth show and I started to say the Shema and I hear somebody saying it, I look over and it's Justin: he memorised it. And now, every show he says it with us.'

Disappointingly for Israeli Beliebers, Justin didn't visit the country during his Believe Tour in 2012/2013 but they hope he will come back soon.

CHAPTER 17

ITALY

B efore Justin visited Italy for the first time, Italian Beliebers campaigned alongside Beliebers from other countries to encourage him to visit them. They held flash mobs and Bieber Parades, and videos from the events were put together to form one seven-minute video entitled 'Bieber Parades & Gathers – How much Beliebers love Justin Bieber'. Make sure you check it out on YouTube: it includes Beliebers from Italy, Chile, Sweden, Portugal, the Netherlands, the Philippines, Malaysia, Denmark, Brazil, Norway and Switzerland.

Justin performed his My World Tour concert in Italy on 9 April 2011 and his Believe Tour on 23 March 2013. He also visited Italy in June 2012 and performed 'Boyfriend' on the TV show *Lo spettacolo sta per iniziare*, which sees the best Italian opera stars and international singers perform onstage and is watched by over 4 million people. He also held a mini-concert to promote his album *Believe* at the Alcatraz venue, Milan.

Justin can speak a small amount of Italian and during one interview said, 'Hello, girls, how are you?' He loves how happy and smiley Italian Beliebers are (and how loud they can be!).

DID YOU KNOW?

Justin won the Best Look Award at the 2012 TRL Awards in Italy, beating Avril Lavigne, Lady Gaga, Marco Mengoni and Nicki Minaj.

When interviewed in Italy, Justin said that performing is the best part of his job and that he loves to be with his fans. He also admitted that he always has lie-ins – unless there is a reason why he has to get up early. Occasionally, he has bad days when he is feeling too lazy and not in the mood, but that is just normal: everyone has days like that.

If you are an Italian Belieber, you should join the Justin Bieber Italia fan page on Facebook. It has over

40,000 fans and reports on the latest Justin news and fan events.

ILENIA'S STORY

Ilenia is seventeen and from Milan. She has been a Belieber since 2010. Her favourite three songs are 'Never Let You Go', 'Common Denominator' and 'Believe'. She explains: 'Every time I listen to them I cry like a baby because they mean so much to me and nobody can understand how they make me feel.' She loves being an Italian Belieber because there is a lot of support for Justin – 'We do Bieber Parades and Street teams, we have so much fun at meetings singing his songs. When he visits Italy, we have two aims: to make him happy and to make him remember us.'

Ilenia met Justin on 25 February 2013 in Bologna. She also saw Kenny Hamilton and Justin's grand-parents, Diane and Bruce Dale. Ilenia says: 'His voice was like an angel's. Everything about him is perfect: his smile, his voice, his skin, his arms, everything. The only thing that I was able to say/scream was, "I love you Justin." I don't know if he heard what I said or if he understood but I didn't care because I was happy and cried with other Beliebers who I didn't even know. I spent the next two hours listening to his voice. It was the best day of my whole life; I want to thank

Justin because he made me feel happy and smile. I have no words to explain how much I love Justin Drew Bieber.'

LUDOVICA'S STORY

Sixteen-year-old Ludovica is from Rome. Her favourite three songs are 'Down To Earth', 'Believe' and 'Be Alright'. She is a member of the Facebook group 'Official Italian Belieber' and they meet up every Saturday to chat about Justin and sing his songs.

Ludovica met Justin on 23 March 2013 in Bologna, the only Italian date of his Believe Tour. She had been longing to meet him for four years. She says: 'I was so nervous, and by the time we got to Bologna, my hair was a mess. I didn't have any make-up on and I needed to change my clothes desperately. Bologna is nearly four hours from my home so I had been travelling for a long time; I was also feeling very tense and sick with nerves.

'I had to get changed in the hotel super-fast and then rush to the arena to meet Justin. I saw Kenny [Hamilton] and Justin's grandparents, which was amazing. Justin appeared on his Segway; I couldn't help but cry, I was so happy to finally meet him. When I went over to see him I struggled to talk as I was so in awe. He said, "Hi, sweetie," and all I could say in reply was "Thank you." He looked so handsome, he was wearing sunglasses and a hat, and I could see his tattoos. Meeting him was a dream come true and something I will never forget.'

GAIA'S STORY

Gaia is sixteen and from Milan. Her favourite three songs are 'Never Let You Go', 'As Long As You Love Me' and 'Fall'. She has been a Belieber for three years and is so glad that Justin is still the same down-to-earth boy she first liked. Gaia says: 'I'm impressed how, even though he is always busy, he makes every single Belieber feel special. I ignore the haters who are just jealous because Justin is so talented. I am one of the main three organisers who organise fan events in Italy. Since 2011, I have been organising flash mobs, Bieber Parades, events to promote *Believe* and much more. To view some of the videos we have made, check out my channel on YouTube – Gaia Giannini.

'Here is my story of how I met Justin. On 2 June 2012, all Italian Beliebers had the opportunity to meet Justin if they won a contest. You would win a pass to see him at a Believe party and Meet & Greet, or at his performance at the Arena of Verona. Francesca (one of my friends) won a Believe Party pass and, although I was happy for her, I was gutted that I didn't win.

'Francesca, Alessandra and some of my other Belieber friends encouraged me to not give up but I really didn't think I had a chance. I went along with them to the Alcatraz, which was where the party was, and we lined up with the other winners. Francesca told me, "You will get to go in, Gaia, I'm sure, you will meet him, we will meet him today, trust me." I couldn't help but cry: Justin was in my city but it really looked like I had no chance of meeting him. We tried every way we could to get an extra pass for me [but] couldn't. After waiting for a few hours, a Belieber walked over to me and told me that she had an extra pass to enter the party and she wanted to give me it. In that moment I was the happiest girl in the world. I thanked her so much and then after one hour we immediately went to Linate, the airport. We stayed there for three hours. Then, when the plane landed we met the whole crew – Kenny, Alfredo, Ryan, Dan, Scrappy – everyone except Justin. All the girls who were with us started to scream; we took photos with them, it was fantastic. We couldn't believe we were with the crew, all the people who are so close to Justin. At the airport I went to Scrappy and I told him, "Can you give this letter to Justin? This is the only chance that I have, please!" He accepted and hugged me.

'When I saw him at the hotel later I asked him if

he threw away the letter or what, and he took it from his pocket! When we were in front of the hotel waiting to see Justin, Marisol [an Italian interviewer and presenter] entered. We went to her to ask why she was there and she explained to us that she was there to interview Justin. After a few minutes, she came back out and said, "Gaia, Alessandra, Ilaria, come here!" We went over to her and she told us that she needed three girls to interview Justin on the stage at the Believe Party. We were so surprised about her request and we accepted. After a while she came back out again and told us that she needed another three girls, so we chose Francesca, Arianna and Camilla. Very soon it was time for the party so we followed Marisol and she took us behind the scenes. We were so excited – the man who managed the event told us to not scream, cry or things like that, but we couldn't help it – seeing Justin in real life was hard to take in.

'After Justin had performed, the man called us and we walked on the stage to interview Justin. He was beautiful – I was enchanted – his eyes were shimmering, he was smiling. He gave me a hug and I can honestly say it was the most special moment of my whole life. I had been waiting years for a hug from Justin! He was so sweet with us; he hugged Alessandra, Ilaria, Francesca, Camilla and Arianna too. After we asked Justin some questions, we went behind the scenes with him and had a photo taken. I will never forget how it felt to be close to Justin.'

CHAPTER 18

JAPAN

Justin first visited Japan in April 2010 and went back just a month later. He was surprised to see how many more Beliebers turned up at the Narita International Airport the second time around, tweeting, 'Just witnessed one of the greatest things ever. Landed in TOKYO and over 100 girls were yelling AW CMON at @thatrygood. EPIC!! hahaha.' (@thatrygood is Justin's swagger coach and stylist Ryan Good's Twitter account.)

In September 2010, Japanese Beliebers Mana, Moe, Yayoi, Haru, Yuko, Misaki, Eri, Madoka, Arisa, Karen, Hanami and Shiho made a video for Justin to express how much they love him and how much they were looking forward to seeing him in concert. They listen to Justin's music every day and their favourite songs are 'One Time' and 'Up'. Eri wanted to say thank you to Justin for coming to Japan, and Madoka vowed that she will support him forever, whatever happens.

Justin went back to Japan in October 2010 and performed 'Baby', 'Never Say Never' and 'U Smile' at Tokyo Dome City LaQua Garden. Japanese Beliebers felt so blessed that he had visited them again. When Justin visited Japan in May 2011, as part of his My World Tour, he took time out to meet children who had been affected by the Japanese earthquake and tsunami which had taken place on Friday, 11 March 2011. Also, he gave them first-row seats to his concert and made sure they had a great time. He tweeted: 'Just met some incredible kids who have been thru alot because of the devastation here in Japan. blessed to meet them and proud to know them.

'When you meet kids like that, with all their strength and courage to move on you realize the important things in life.'

DID YOU KNOW?

Justin joined with other huge stars such as Beyoncé, Rihanna, U2 and Madonna for the *Songs For Japan* charity album, which raised over $5 million for the Japanese Red Cross Society. It was released for download on 25 March 2011 and the CD version was released on 4 April 2011. He also donated a proportion of Japan concert ticket sales to the fund and encouraged fans to pray and donate whatever they could.

Justin loves Japan so much that it is his favourite travel destination. He told *Gulf News*: 'I like the culture and they are very, very nice. I like how they bow and take off their shoes when they go to someone's house – it's similar to Canada. In Canada, we take off our shoes when we go to houses. In America, you just walk in with your dirty shoes all over the carpet.'

The capital of Japan, Tokyo, is one of Justin's favourite cities to visit; his other favourites are Sydney in Australia and Los Angeles in America. He loved visiting Tokyo in April 2010. When he was over there, he tweeted: 'only been here a little while and Tokyo is already 1 of my favorite cities.'

Also, 'Exclusive kicks everywhere, great food and heated toilet seats.'

'Just had sushi dinner here in Japan. food was incredible but i didnt know half the stuff i was eating. now gotta adjust to the time zone.'

'About to start interviews here in Japan...working on my Japanese... おやすみなさい。 – That means "Goodnight and sweet dreams" ;-)'

'私はあなたの電話番号を有してもいいか。 – That is "Can I have your phone number?" This line is very important to me while traveling this country. Lol.'

'Got 2 start my interviews here in Tokyo...it's wild being here. Thanks 4 all the love. U guys got me traveling the world and livin a dream.'

Justin visited Japan in July 2012 to promote his *Believe* album and he had a blast. He appeared on the *Sukkiri* TV show and even tried to speak a bit of Japanese, saying, 'Sexy da ne' (which means, 'You're sexy'). He showed off his impressive table tennis skills, too. In another interview, this time on a TV show called *Zip*, Justin wore some funny fake moustaches, and he tried sushi during an interview on the TV show *IITOMO*. Justin didn't just do interviews, though; he performed some songs during his trip to Japan. In Tokyo, he performed 'Boyfriend', 'Baby' and 'Die In Your Arms'; he also did an acoustic version of 'Baby' with Dan Kanter during another mini-concert.

After his trip, Justin recorded a short message for his Japanese fans, saying: 'Hey what's up to all my Japanese fans, I just wanted to say thank you for an amazing trip and believe!'

CHAPTER 19

LUXEMBOURG

Justin has never toured Luxembourg, but if he did then he would make the dreams of his Luxembourg Beliebers come true. Luxembourg is a small country in Europe, with only around half a million inhabitants. It borders France, Germany and Belgium, and its capital city is called Luxembourg.

There is a Justin Bieber Luxembourg Facebook page, which is run by superfan Tina, so, if you are from Luxembourg, it is well worth joining. There might be fewer than 400 fans but the Luxembourg Beliebers are very passionate. Also, there is a 'If you would like a concert of Justin Bieber in Luxembourg' fan page, which is run by a superfan called Sarah. She says: 'Maybe you don't know where the hell Luxembourg is.

Well, it's a veryyyy small country in Europe! Right beside Germany! We have our own concert hall & we're very proud of it. People like Katy Perry, Lady Gaga, Tokio Hotel [and] The Pussycat Dolls have already performed here but the most important person of all hasn't performed here yet: Justin Bieber! Please, help us little Luxembourgish Beliebers to get him here! We love him so much! But, I guess he don't even know that our country exists): so PLEASE sign up & help us to get Justin Bieber to Luxembourg & give a concert! That would be so AMAZING.'

MARIA'S STORY

Maria is sixteen and from Luxembourg. Her favourite three songs are 'Down To Earth', 'Be Alright' and 'Fall'. As already mentioned, Justin has never been to Luxembourg but Maria hopes he will one day. It is hard for Beliebers there to get hold of merchandise and magazines featuring him.

Maria met Justin in Frankfurt, Germany, which is a six-hour drive from her home. She says: 'I've been a Belieber for four years now. I remember watching Justin's music video "One Time" on YouTube and instantly falling in love with him. Since then my life has changed. Justin was the very first artist I supported, and I doubt that I will ever support any other artist like I support him. Justin's music has helped me through so much and has kept me going every day. Since I live in a very small country, not many artists come here. I couldn't attend Justin's first tour and I was hoping that maybe on his next one he would come here. My parents know how much Justin means to me so they said that they would take me to another country just so I could see Justin. I started saving money and, a few months before the new tour dates were coming out, I joined Justin's official website so I could get a pre-sale code to make sure I would get tickets. Finally, after so many years of waiting, I got tickets to see Justin in Frankfurt, Germany on April 3rd.

'My tickets were right in front of the stage! I remember crying so much after I bought them – I still couldn't believe it was happening, I was finally going to see Justin! My friend also bought a ticket so I wouldn't go all by myself. I'd been a member of *Bieberfever* [Justin's official website] for a year and I saw that there was a contest for each show of the tour to win Meet & Greets. I obviously entered the contest for the date of my show. Honestly, I'm a very negative person, and I barely win anything, but this time I did everything I could to win. Justin taught me to always believe that anything's possible, that dreams do come true, to never say never. Since I was going to see Justin in Germany, we left the day before the concert. The next morning I opened the email, and I couldn't believe what I was reading: "Congratulations Maria, you're officially invited to attend the photo meet & greet tomorrow night April 3rd in Frankfurt..." I seriously stood there looking at it for a few minutes. I couldn't believe I had won the contest, it felt like a dream. I started crying and called my friend, saying that we were going to meet Justin!

'Finally, the day I was waiting the most [for] arrived: April 3rd. My friend and I went straight to the arena. I'd never been there before, and I didn't know where the ticket box office was, where I was supposed to get my wristbands for the Meet & Greet. Plus I didn't know how to speak German so that made things more difficult. I met an amazing German Belieber, who helped translate so I could speak to the security guards to try and get more information about the Meet & Greet wristbands, but no one knew anything. We waited till 4pm. It was freezing cold in Frankfurt, and waiting so long outside was horrible, but it was worth it. After all the people with priority got in, it was the turn for the others. That's when they told me that I was supposed to get my wristbands in the ticket box office, which was near the normal entrance, at the opposite side to where I was. I started running so fast, I swear I never ran that fast during my whole life. Finally, I got my wristbands.

'While waiting, I met this girl that I had spoken to on Twitter. Meeting Beliebers is the best thing ever. She told me that Dan Kanter was there and that she got a picture with him! I turned around and saw Dan Kanter taking pictures with basically every single person that was there. I went up to him and we hugged and had a photo together. Then it was time to meet Justin. Since I hadn't bought the Meet & Greet, I had to be in a picture of six people. I was praying that I had the chance to stand next to Justin. He was standing there, a few metres away from me, the real Justin Drew Bieber!

'When it was my turn, I was lucky enough to be in a group of four people and stood right next to him. I'm not sure if I said "Hi" or not, I was so speechless and I couldn't believe what was happening. Justin looked a bit serious but his face was so flawless, so perfect, and gorgeous. Words can't even describe it. I was standing next to him and he had his arm around my friend and I. I was touching Justin, I was in the same room as him; I was taking a picture with him, I was living a dream! After two seconds, the security guard pushed me away, and I didn't even have time to ask for a hug. I was so overcome with emotion, I broke down crying.'

Because the Meet & Greets were running late, Maria had to go straight to her seat because Justin was about to go onstage. Her seat was in the front row so she had the perfect view. She adds: 'As soon as the countdown hit 00:00, that's when the magic started. The show was incredibly amazing, Justin's voice was perfect – everything was perfect. I was so close to the stage; Justin was just a few metres away, it was unreal! While singing "Eenie Meenie", Justin went in front of my friends and I and pointed at the three of us. But everything good comes to an end, and the show was over. To be honest, it went by so fast, it felt like ten minutes! It was the best experience of my life. I started crying so much while walking out of the arena and going to the hotel. It was all over and I was so grateful for everything that happened. I got to meet Justin, go to his concert, I couldn't ask for anything more.

'I guess Justin's right: dreams DO come true. To every one of you that thinks that dreams don't come true, that it's impossible to meet Justin, don't ever give up: keep trying. You just have to fight for it, and never say never. My dream came true, yours can too.'

CHAPTER 20

MALAYSIA

Malaysian Beliebers performed a purple flash mob on 19 April 2011 at the Pavilion shopping centre in the Bukit Bintang district of Kuala Lumpur. The choreography was excellent and the Beliebers spent a long time practising to get everything perfect. To find the video just search for 'Justin Bieber flash mob Malaysia' on YouTube, it is well worth a watch. Malaysian Beliebers also have their own website, *www.justinbiebermalaysia.webs.com*, so they can chat online and organise projects and events.

Justin performed his My World Tour concert in Kuala Lumpur at the Stadium Merdeka on 21 April 2011. It was a special outdoors show, with Good Charlotte's Joel Madden joining Justin onstage.

Justin thoroughly enjoyed himself despite the rain and even jumped off the stage. The next day he tweeted: 'Yeah i jumped in the crowd last night...had to. It was a party.'

During his visit, he stayed at the Kuala Lumpur Hilton hotel and enjoyed trying traditional Malaysian food such as nasi goreng, satay and nasi lemak and drinking guava juice.

Sadly, Justin didn't perform his Believe Tour concert in the country but he visited again in July 2012 to perform at the MTV World Stage Live. He was joined by South Korean girl band KARA, Malaysian singer Mizz Nina and Korean rapper/dancer Jay Park. Justin performed 'Die In Your Arms', 'All Around The World' and 'Boyfriend'. The crowd of 15,000 music fans went wild.

DID YOU KNOW?

Justin went surfing before the MTV World Stage Live, tweeting his followers a photo and the message: 'Just surfin like a beast lol.' He also revealed: 'Excited to be back in Malaysia for MTV World Stage! But first a day off playing some games and chillin by the pool.'

Justin also managed to do some shopping in the Wangsa Walk Mall, which must have been nice because usually he gets mobbed whenever he attempts to go shopping in other countries. While in Malaysia, he held a South East Asia Press Conference for his *Believe* album at Sunway Pyramid shopping centre. He told the host: 'I recorded *My World* in, like, three weeks so, like, with this album I wanted to really be involved more, and we spent like eight to nine months recording it, so [it] was a lot different... more of a process, and I felt definitely more involved. I worked with so many different producers and basically... and different writers too... it's 100 per cent me.'

On 2 February 2013, Malaysian Beliebers held their first Justin Bieber buy-out. They met at the Suria KLCC shopping centre and bought as many *Believe Acoustic* CDs as they could for the Make-A-Wish Foundation. To see a great video capturing what Malaysian Beliebers got up to that day, go to YouTube and search for 'Justin Bieber Buy-Out Fans Gathering in Malaysia'.

CHAPTER 21

MEXICO

Justin performed his My World Tour concert in Mexico on 30 September 2011 in Monterrey and in Mexico City on 1 and 2 October 2011. Tickets for the shows sold out in just two hours, leaving many Mexican Beliebers devastated. One fan was filmed sobbing on the floor and, when Justin saw the clip the day before his concert on 30 September, he decided that he had to find out who she was. He tweeted: 'Need everyone's help. we have LESS than 24 hours. we need to find this girl...she is at the 30 sec mark. HELP! thanks.'

Thankfully, Beliebers managed to name the girl and she got to go to the concert. Her name was Debanhi Guzman Torres and she was so happy to receive two tickets to the show. Justin is so kind to have tracked Debanhi down and he chose her to be his 'One Less Lonely Girl' that night, which meant that he serenaded her onstage!

For his Mexico shows, the opening acts were boy band Big Time Rush and dance-pop band Cobra Starship. Justin had a great time and loved it when fans waited for him outside his hotel, and he tweeted, 'MEXICO CITY!! I can hear the fans outside the hotel. #MUCHLOVE – TE AMO MUCHO!'

Two months after his concerts, in December 2011, Justin visited Mexico to attend the beach wedding of a friend of the actress Selena Gomez. He really enjoyed himself, taking time out to relax by a swimming pool and going jet skiing too.

DID YOU KNOW?

In October 2011, Justin was presented with two special discs, one for his *My World* album going three times Platinum and the other for *Never Say Never* going Gold.

Mexican Beliebers were thrilled when it was announced that Justin would be performing three concerts in their country as part of his Believe Tour.

He performed in Mexico City on 18, 19 and 20 November 2013 to sell-out crowds.

On 11 June 2012, Justin received a special plaque during a press conference for *Believe* at the W Hotel, Mexico City. The plaque was to commemorate Justin selling half a million records in Mexico alone – what an achievement! That night he celebrated with 300,000 Beliebers at a free outdoor concert at Zócalo Square. Some fans camped for two days to make sure they were as close to the stage as possible. The crowd were so loud, singing at the tops of their voices with Justin as he performed 'Baby'.

In a backstage video Justin recorded for Beliebers, he revealed: 'I never thought I could be loved this much, I never thought that I would have so many people who just want to hear my music, hear me sing and I can't say how thankful I am. I can't say how thankful I am that at least one of you cared enough to write messages to me on Twitter, to write when I get sick, when I get hurt...'

When he posted up the video, he wrote: 'I shot this on my phone backstage in Mexico City before the show tonight. Put on a free show and 300,000 people showed up. A lot of emotions but just wanted to say I wouldn't be here without all of your support. Wanted you to know how I feel. Thanks for everything. I hope you chase every dream as you are helping me live mine every day. thank you.'

In December 2012, after Justin had celebrated Christmas, he decided to fly in a private jet to Mexico for New Year. He stayed in Puerto Vallarta, Jalisco, Mexico and tweeted his followers a photograph of himself without a top on and the message: 'Enjoying the sun in Mexico.'

If you are a Mexican Belieber, make sure you become a fan of 'Justin Bieber Mexico' on Facebook – the page is liked by over 80,000 people!

CHAPTER 22

THE NETHERLANDS

On 27 March 2011, Justin performed his My World Tour concert in Rotterdam and his Believe Tour concert in Arnhem on 13 April 2013.

Justin revealed that his life hasn't changed that much when interviewed by *NOS.nl* in 2010. He said: 'Not a lot has changed, other than the fact I am able to travel the world and see some great things.' He also confessed that he uses past experiences of relationships when writing songs, but sometimes it is storytelling rather than being based on actual things that have happened to him.

> **DID YOU KNOW?**
>
> One Dutch fan asked what was the craziest thing that a fan has done and Justin replied that it was getting tattoos of his song lyrics.

When Justin was in Amsterdam in April 2013, he took time out from his busy schedule to visit the Hermitage Museum. He also visited the Anne Frank Museum the day before his concert, and staff there were thrilled that he had stopped by, saying a few days later: 'The Anne Frank House was pleased to welcome Justin Bieber to the Anne Frank House last Friday. We think it is very positive that he took the time and effort to visit our museum. He was very interested in the story of Anne Frank and stayed for over an hour. We hope that his visit will inspire his fans to learn more about her life and hopefully read the diary.'

FENNA'S STORY

Fenna is sixteen and from Maarssen. Her favourite three songs (at the moment) are 'Fall', 'Catching Feelings' and 'Down To Earth'. She says: 'What I love the most about Justin is that he encourages his fans to follow their dreams. He teaches us that we should never give up because dreams do come true. And I think he really proves that with his own story, because he came from nowhere busking on the streets and now he's on top of the world. My dream was to meet Justin and I never gave up. Furthermore I love his smile, I love to see him happy doing what he loves the most.

'Being a Belieber in my country is quite hard but I don't really think it matters really which country you live in, being a Belieber is hard anyway. We get judged a lot, not only on the internet but also at school. People will always judge you for being a Belieber, which I don't understand – other fanbases don't get judged like we do. And I think everyone should have someone that makes them follow their dreams and be who they want to be, and, for me, that's Justin. I don't understand how you can be judgemental on someone or something that is an inspiration to someone else. They don't understand how Justin saved many lives by doing what he does.

'I have been to EVERY SINGLE Belieber meeting and Bieber Parade in the Netherlands. The first one was on 7 October 2010. It was kind of awkward because it was the first Bieber Parade ever and I didn't meet any of the girls and boys beforehand but it turned out really nice; I met a lot of people, we did a flash mob, sang and danced a lot. We went shouting through the streets of Utrecht and we had a lot of fun. I've been to, like, over fifteen of these meetings now and it's really fun. I have made a lot of great friends because of Justin. I have a group-chat with about ten other Beliebers and, although we live all around the country, we try to meet as often as possible and we try to visit for each other's birthdays. I'm really thankful to Justin because, without him, I wouldn't have known these girls.

'I've been a huge fan of Justin since the beginning. People at school often say I'm obsessed and sometimes judge me for it, but I don't really care and keep supporting Justin. I went to my first concert on 27 March 2013 and it was amazing! Unfortunately, I didn't get the chance to meet him – I never thought about being able to meet Justin because it seemed so unreal. However, in November 2011 I got diagnosed with cancer (I'm cured now). Although I went through a really hard time, I never gave up and kept going. My hospital told me I was allowed to do a wish at the Make-A-Wish Foundation. For everyone who doesn't know what that is, the mission of Make-A-Wish International is to grant the wishes of children with life-threatening medical conditions to enrich their human experience with hope, strength and joy. When I was told that I could make a wish, I didn't even have to think about it: I wanted to meet

Justin Bieber. They came over to my house and asked literally EVERYTHING about me. They said they would try to make my wish come true but I had to be patient.

'In May 2012, the Believe Tour dates came out and Justin was coming to Holland! I couldn't believe it, but, since Make-A-Wish didn't guarantee a Meet & Greet, I didn't know if I would be going to the concert. I bought golden circle tickets and had really good seats! I was really happy about that; however, I did tell my friend there was a chance I couldn't go with her because maybe I would go with Make-A-Wish. Later, Make-A-Wish rang us to tell us it was going to happen, although after that I had to wait quite a long time to know the exact date. I was so happy and I told everyone about it, although I felt sorry for my friend that I couldn't go to the concert with her. I sold my ticket to her mum so she didn't have to go alone. At first she was sad and I think a little bit angry at the same time, but, the night before the concert, she won a Meet & Greet too! Finally, on 13 April 2013 at 10am in the morning, I got picked up in a pink limousine. I was taken to Zara to choose some new clothes and I got a Nikon camera! We went to a hair salon and they did my hair and make-up, which made me feel like a star. Finally, we went to GelreDome, where the concert would take place.

'Justin arrived at around 9pm, and the Meet & Greets started. I was told I had to go last, so we could have the most time. I saw a lot of girls coming out of the Meet & Greets, including my friends. I had to wait backstage behind a curtain so I shouted to my friends to ask them how he looked; they said he was perfect and what he was wearing. This made me even more nervous. After waiting a couple of minutes I had to go in the back of the line. Every time someone came out, I saw Justin for a second and my heart almost dropped. They told us we were allowed to take our own pictures and I had no idea how long I could stay there.

'When it was finally my turn, I went in the room and looked Justin in his eyes. He was like, "Hey, sweetie," and then everything went so fast. Justin asked me if I wanted to take pictures so I took my iPhone out of my pocket and he was like, "Ah, selfies!" We took a picture and he said, "Let me give you a kiss" and he kissed my cheek. After that I gave him my letter and Dutch "stroopwafels". Justin said, "THESE ARE SO GOOD, I LOVE DUTCH WAFFLES," and he gave me a hug. Justin then signed my shirt and book, and said I could have asked for more, but I was satisfied. My mother, my father and my brother were there too because I could take my family. My father and brother gave him a handshake and my mum gave him a hug and wanted a picture as well – it was so cute because my mum is a huge Justin fan too. Justin gave me another hug, I said, "This feels so good," and he said, "Aw, I love you, sweetheart."

'He had to leave and I held him super-tight. I don't really know what else to say, I got to spend like five to ten minutes and these moments were probably the most exciting of my life. When Justin looked at me, he looked so deep in my eyes and it was so unreal. Now, my pictures are all over Twitter and Tumblr, which is quite weird because I used to look at these pics from other girls but now it's ME! I really want to thank Make-A-Wish for my perfect day. I had the time of my life and I seriously will never forget meeting Justin.'

KIM'S STORY

Fifteen-year-old Kim is from Zoetermeer. Her favourite songs are 'One Less Lonely Girl', 'Boyfriend' and 'I Would'. Kim is the only Belieber in her school but she has lots of Belieber friends on Twitter. She says: 'I love to talk with Beliebers because I feel like they understand me. We have Belieber meetings once or twice a year and it's just really fun because we talk about Justin Bieber all day and sing his songs.'

Kim has been supporting Justin since the beginning and would watch his videos on YouTube before he got a record deal. In 2010, she and her dad went all the way to New York to see Justin perform live. She explains what happened: 'After the (perfect) concert, the people from Island Def Jam [Music] Group were so surprised and honoured that I had travelled so far for Justin that they sang "Happy Birthday" to me because it was my 13th birthday just a few days later. They were all super-sweet and I gave them a letter for Justin.

'February 21st was the first time I saw Justin and it was perfect. Then in 2011, I went back to New York. Justin wasn't there at that time, but I went to see his management again at Def Jam. They had moved to another location and, because Justin was more popular, I couldn't get in the building any more. The second time I saw Justin was in Holland in 2012. He was so handsome and I couldn't believe we were breathing the same air. The third time I met him was in the Netherlands on 13 April 2013. I had hoped to get a hug and a kiss but I was so awestruck I didn't get the chance to ask him. I can't wait to see him again next time he comes to the Netherlands.'

LIZZY'S STORY

Lizzy is eighteen and from Ter Aar. Her favourite three songs are 'That Should Be Me', 'Fall' and 'Beauty And A Beat'. She thinks it's hard being a

Belieber in the Netherlands because 'there are a lot of Justin Bieber haters here, but it's worth it and there's also a lot of Beliebers here. A few times a year we hold Belieber meetings and we're like one big family – it feels like everyone has known each other for years. We sometimes do flash mobs at our meetings, which are great fun, and, in July 2013, me and three other Beliebers organised a meeting at Walibi World Amusement Park.'

Lizzy met Justin in Belgium at the Antwerps Sportpaleis. She couldn't get tickets for his concert in the Netherlands because they sold out too fast but managed to convince her mum to buy herself and her sister Meet & Greet tickets for the Belgium show, after promising she would pay her back.

Lizzy takes up the story: 'After buying the tickets I had to wait 279 days, but time went by so fast. I couldn't sleep the night before the big day because I was so nervous. Me and my sister went to Belgium with a Belieber I had met on Twitter. Before the Meet & Greet, [guitarist] Dan Kanter walked in. I said, "Can I get a hug?" and he said, "Of course!" Then I took my phone and took a picture with him. I said, "Thank you, I love you so much." He was so sweet and little. We also heard the crowd (the arena was above us). The Meet & Greets started and I sprayed Justin's perfume "Girlfriend" everywhere.

'I saw Justin between the curtains; I started to cry. I walked over to Justin in the room and it was so dark I couldn't see him very well. There were no lights and it was surrounded with black curtains. He said, "Hi, sweetheart." He was so perfect, so sweet, so little and so cute. I was standing next to him, my heart was beating so fast and they took a picture. I said, "I love you so much!" and he smiled. The security guard pushed me away. I walked out and I broke down in tears. I never cried like that before, everyone was looking at me. I saw my sister standing in the row; she started to cry too because of me.

'I saw the girl who had met him before me and we cried together. We hugged each other a lot. Then we started to walk into the arena and I couldn't stop crying. Everyone was staring at me. I almost fell down the stairs because I was shaking. I was sitting at the second row. My sister came over to me and we hugged each other, we couldn't stop crying. The concert was perfect and I took a lot of pictures and videos.'

ELSEMIEKE'S STORY

Sixteen-year-old Elsemieke is from Waalwijk. She has been a Belieber for four years. Her favourite three songs are 'Christmas Eve', 'Favorite Girl' and 'As Long As You Love Me'. She says: 'It's amazing to be a Belieber. Sometimes I get hate or people laugh at me because I am a little obsessed, lol, but I think that happens to fans in every country. There are a lot of Beliebers here in the Netherlands – we always go to Belieber meetings, where we can all come together and have fun.' Elsemieke likes taking part in fan videos for Justin and, when she travelled with her friends to see Justin on tour, they took special banners to hold up during the different songs. When he sang 'Believe', they held up banners saying 'We Believe'.

Elsemieke met Justin at the GelreDome football stadium in the city of Arnhem, in the Netherlands on 13 April 2013. She burst into tears as soon as she saw Justin, she couldn't believe she was meeting him. He gave her a hug and said, 'Thank you, sweet loving,' when she thanked him and told him she loved him. She hopes she will get to meet him again one day.

DIANA'S STORY

Nineteen-year-old Diana is from Doetinchem. She has been a Belieber since she saw the 'One Less Lonely Girl' video. Her favourite three songs are 'Overboard', 'Love Me Like You Do' and 'Believe'. Diana also met Justin on 13 April 2013 at the GelreDome football stadium. She went backstage with her friend and a camera crew, who filmed the experience. The camera crew had filmed her getting ready and interviewed her too.

Diana says: 'When I walked over to Justin, I wanted to say "Hi" or something, but I forgot how to talk. Justin grabbed my waist and pulled me closer. I looked at him, then at the camera. Suddenly I noticed Justin was holding my scarf and was playing with it. I just watched and it was so cute! He said, "I like it." I had so much to say, but not a word left my mouth. He had a big smile and you could hear him giggle. I was pulled away by a security guard but I just let him, I was so shocked.'

VITA'S STORY

Vita is sixteen and from Kockengen. Her three favourite songs are 'Fall', 'Down To Earth' and 'Beauty And A Beat'. She says: 'I love how Justin can always find a way to put a smile on my face. His amazing voice and beautiful smile can light up my world every day. And I love the way he treats his Beliebers!'

Vita met Justin on 13 April 2013: 'He looked even more flawless than I could ever have expected; the first thing I saw were his sexy muscles and his tattoos. We had to get ready for the picture so I laid my hand on his back on purpose. I was just standing there, staring at Justin. He suddenly looked me in the eyes and I wanted to hug him so bad, I reached out my hand for him! He grabbed my hand and tried to pull me closer to him, but the security guard was already trying to pull me away.

'Justin was still holding my hand and said the words I'll never forget, "I love you, sweetie." After that he winked at me and did his sexy nod (aka smile). My jaw dropped even more and, with that last smile, the security guard pulled my arm so Justin had to let go. I turned around while looking at Justin for the last time. "I love you so much, Justin," I said. I was crying and breathing heavily. Some random Beliebers came to hug me and were crying with me because they were so happy for me. They kept saying things like, "You deserved it so much, I'm so happy for you." Beliebers really are the best fans in the world!'

CHAPTER 23

NEW ZEALAND

Justin loves visiting New Zealand and meeting his Kiwi Beliebers. He didn't have the opportunity to perform his My World Tour concert in the country but he did perform his Believe Tour concert on 23 and 24 November 2013 in Auckland.

When Justin flew into New Zealand in April 2010, his life was put at risk when he was mobbed by over-excited fans; he had no option but to try to get out of the airport as quickly as possible. Poor Pattie was knocked over and two Beliebers stole Justin's hat. The Beliebers hadn't set out to upset Justin, his family or the crew, but had just been caught up in the moment of seeing their hero in person for the first time.

Justin tweeted the next day: 'Finally got to New

Zealand last night. The airport was crazy. Not happy that someone stole my hat and knocked down my mama. Come on people. I want to be able to sign and take pics and meet my fans, but if you are all pushing security won't let me. Let's keep it safe and have fun.'

Beliebers were shocked about what had happened to Pattie and she received many messages asking if she was okay. She tweeted back: 'Thanks for all ur support!! I'm ok thank you!!!'

The girls who had stolen Justin's hat had thought that having it would give them an excuse to see Justin again so they could give it back, but he didn't want to meet up with them. He gave a journalist from 3 News this message for the girls: 'You stole my property. It's essentially illegal. But it's fine, I forgive you – I love you.'

Justin later tweeted: 'Sorry, you can't hold me ransom. I got my hat back. No hugs, no thank u's. Just glad they did the right thing. I don't condone thievery!! Haha.'

DID YOU KNOW?

During Justin's 2010 trip to New Zealand, he tried a bottle of fizzy water but didn't like the taste and so he threw it away, but someone picked it up and managed to sell it for $683 online. The money raised went to the Australian charity CanTeen, which supports young people with cancer.

Justin and Pattie both decided to bungee jump off Auckland Bridge, an experience they will never forget. Afterwards, Justin tweeted: 'NEW ZEALAND = GREAT SUCCESS (Borat voice).'

In July 2012, he visited New Zealand again. He performed acoustically for Kiwi fans and, when complimented on his performance the next day by a presenter from ZM TV, he said: 'Thank you so much, it's something I love and it definitely brings me back to, you know, where I started and I started performing acoustically on the street and on YouTube for my fans so, you know, it's cool to be able to do that.'

Justin also got the opportunity to meet some members of the New Zealand Rugby Union side during his visit. He posed for a photo with locks Ali Williams and Anthony Boric, who both stand at 6ft 7in (2 metres). Poor Justin looked tiny, standing next to them with his signed rugby shirt! Justin made sure he also took time out to visit the Starship Children's Hospital in Auckland (he always tries to visit hospitals in the different countries he visits because he likes to give something back).

Justin really wanted to spend longer in New Zealand but he had to fly back to America for the Teen Choice Awards as he was due to perform 'Boyfriend' and 'As Long As You Love Me' there.

Kiwi fans are so dedicated that they have their own website: *www.justinbiebernz.com*.

CHAPTER 24

NORWAY

Norwegian Beliebers held a Bieber Parade in Oslo on 13 August 2011 to encourage Justin to visit their country. They were thrilled when they found out that he had seen the video they had made of the event, just an hour after it was posted up. He tweeted: 'Oslo goes hard. thank you. keep in touch with the fans… never forget who got you here….always show love. #thisisafamily #REAL.'

Justin didn't visit Norway as part of his My World Tour but he did perform his Believe Tour in Fornebu, Bærum from 16 to 18 April 2013. He also made a short promotional visit in May 2012, which included a mini-concert in Oslo.

At the mini-concert, so many Beliebers turned up

that the security team struggled to cope. Forty-nine fans were injured and fourteen ended up being taken to hospital in ambulances. The show was almost cancelled by police but thankfully went ahead after Justin tweeted fans to ask them to try to stay calm. He wrote: 'Norway – please listen to the police. I dont want anyone getting hurt. I want everything to go to plan but your safety must come first.'

Although Justin's press conference was cancelled for security reasons, he was interviewed by individual members of the press, including the Norwegian talk-show host Fredrik Skavlan. While being interviewed by Fredrik, he decided to talk about a crazy experience that happened when he was seven years old. Justin was camping with his family in a cabin in the North of Canada when he woke up early and decided to head outside. He revealed: 'I had a stick and I was moving the fire around, and I was waiting for my grandparents to wake up and, all of a sudden, I see a bear – like a big bear, literally, like, ten feet away from me in the garbage – and I'm only, like, seven so I don't really know the danger that I'm really in right now, so I run inside and I'm, like, "Grandma, Grandpa, there's a bear outside!"'

It turned out that the bear had been causing trouble in the community for a while, so permission had been granted for it to be shot. Justin's grandparents ended up ringing Justin's uncle, who drove to the lodge, shot the bear and then they all ate it.

Justin concluded: 'My family were a bunch of hillbillies and I ate bear!'

DID YOU KNOW?

Justin and Dan Kanter performed 'Be Alright' for fans during the Norwegian trip – a song they had written together in Bali, Indonesia.

When Justin was due to visit Norway in April 2013, five schools decided that it would be best if they changed the dates of their midterm exams so that Beliebers wouldn't skip them in order to make it to one of his Oslo concerts. Kristin Halvorsen, Norway's education minister, told the press: 'I am concerned that students should be concentrating when they take tests and midterms. The local schools have the responsibility to schedule the local midterms, and, if they think there is any reason to change the dates, they have authority to do so.

'We've all been fourteen years old and know that interests can be intense.'

While in Norway, Justin performed on a boat but

when he went to leave he had eighty other boats following him – something he hasn't experienced anywhere else. He is used to the paparazzi and fans following him in cars, but not in boats!

DID YOU KNOW?

Before Justin goes onstage he says a prayer with his crew, and then they all chant, 'Ducks, ducks, ducks, ducks, quack, quack, quack, quack.' The chant is from the 1992 ice hockey movie *The Mighty Ducks*.

Before his show on 17 April 2013, Justin was presented with a special plaque from Universal Music Group in Oslo, celebrating his album sales. He loved it and tweeted a photo of the giant plaque to fans, with the message: 'Just got this! Thank u Norway. Gonna be a great show tonight!'

People think that being Justin and getting to travel the world is easy, but it's not. Justin has to work long hours and often he doesn't get any time to explore the different cities. He explained how travelling far from home impacts on him to the *Guardian*: 'You're so far away and you start feeling like you're a robot. When I'm overseas the schedule is always crazy and then there's the time change and you're not even yourself. It's weird.'

Norwegian fans should check out the Justin Bieber Norway page on Facebook.

HEIDI'S STORY

Heidi is seventeen and from Vennesla. Her favourite three songs are 'Believe', 'Be Alright' and 'Down To Earth'. She says: 'To be a Belieber in Norway is really fun, even though you get funny looks from your classmates because you're a Belieber. Justin has been in my country a couple of times and the media blows it up so much, like how the Beliebers are overreacting when he's here and that makes it seem like most Beliebers are crazy, which is not the case at all. Beliebers are some of the nicest people I've ever met and I've made so many friends, even best friends through Justin.'

Heidi met Justin at the Telenor Arena in Bærum on 18 April 2013. She reveals how it came about: 'As with every Belieber, it's been my dream to meet Justin. My best friend decided to start the hashtag #BieberMeetHeidi on Twitter. She wrote on Twitter about it and spread the word. We got a lot of accounts tweeting about it, but that wasn't enough. As it came closer and closer to the concert, I tweeted the crew about the hashtag. I also had entered Bieberfever's

Best Collection contest a few weeks earlier which involved sending in a photograph of my bedroom with all my posters and merchandise on display.

'On the 17th I was a nervous wreck all day long, and I had my phone with me because I knew Bieberfever was going to email whoever won their competition. My best friend came over to my house in the evening and we were just chilling when I suddenly got an email. It was from Bieberfever saying that I've won the contest and I was gonna meet Justin. I jumped up and down screaming, "I'M MEETING JUSTIN! I WON!" My friend was like, "Haha, you're so funny," but then I started crying and she realised I wasn't kidding. I then called my other best friend because I was going to the concert with both of them the next day and I was allowed to bring one friend to the Meet & Greet. I couldn't pick between them, so I decided to write down each one of their names on a piece of paper and then pick one, because that was the only fair way to decide. I decided to email Bieberfever, asking them if there was any way possible that I could get an extra Meet & Greet pass so my other friend wouldn't be walking alone at the arena. They replied to say that they would put in the request.

'The next day we were outside at the waiting area at the arena for four hours and it was so cold outside. When the clock hit 4pm, it was time for the Meet &

Greet people to walk into the arena. I asked the people for a third wristband but that wasn't enough for them. Lena and I had no other choice to leave Lene in the waiting area inside the building. We went to another room, waiting to get the information we needed to meet Justin. Suddenly, Lene came in crying – with a wristband on! We all cried a bit because we were so happy that all of us were going to meet Justin. There was a table outside the room where you could put down gifts you had for Justin, and I had written him a letter. Suddenly the whole line moved really fast, and it was our turn to meet Justin! When the security guard held the curtain open to let the people who were meeting Justin before us in, I saw Justin. I said to my friends, "There he is! I just saw him!" and then it was our turn.

'I looked straight at Justin's face, not a single flaw – he really is as perfect as he looks like in pictures, he's even more flawless in real life if that's even possible. The security guards were like, "Okay, you go there, and you there, and smile," and then the photo was taken. Right after the photo was taken, the security guards were pushing us out, but I managed to ask Justin something as I walked past him. "Can I get a hug?" I asked, and he answered, "No, sorry." Turns out they were all in a hurry and they were behind schedule. While Justin was saying, "No, sorry," he looked genuinely sad. I'm not even kidding – my friends also saw it, it broke my heart. The fact that he replied to my question, he heard what I said and he answered made my day, it made my year. He talked to me. When we were outside the arena I was just like, whoa, did I just meet Justin Bieber, my idol, my inspiration and hero? Yes!

'I just want to tell whoever reads this, never say never and believe in your dreams. I was so close to giving up, but I didn't and I met him. Enter every competition and tweet the crew and Beliebers. It's worth a try!'

JULIANNE'S STORY

Seventeen-year-old Julianne is from Trondheim. Her favourite three songs are 'Never Let You Go', 'As Long As You Love Me' and 'Fall'. She says: 'It's amazing being a Norwegian Belieber – we are very crazy, lovely and funny. Norway is a little and boring country, so when a big celebrity comes here, like Justin, the whole country goes crazy! Justin came to Norway for the first time on his promo tour, and the capital Oslo literally got turned upside down. No other celebrity has made such a huge impact on our country. People were going crazy, running down the streets and right into the traffic, screaming and singing. And I have to admit I was one of them, and it was so much fun! We just wanted to do anything we could to see him, because we didn't know if or when he was going to come back here. He held an amazing free show – it was incredible! Justin was performing on a boat on the water, and we were as close as we could be. I will never forget that day. (I have to say that it's also amazing to see Oslo in the "All Around The World" music video.)

'Then almost a year later, it was time for a new Bieber adventure. Believe Tour came to Oslo on April 16th 2013. In July, my sister and I were lucky enough to buy the best tickets, which included Meet & Greet passes, diamond circle tickets and merchandise. While we were waiting in the Meet & Greet line, Dan Kanter and Nick DeMoura from Justin's crew came by. I got up and spoke to them, and they were so nice. I was really looking forward to meeting Justin but, in the same way, I didn't have any big expectations because I'd heard that the meetings would go by very fast. I know that the security guards have to do their job – I just wish they could've been more sympathetic and treat us like human beings. Even though I didn't manage to say or do what I wanted to do, the seconds I had with Justin meant the world to me. When I got in and saw him, he looked so magical and unreal. His skin and tattoos were literally shining – I've never seen someone that beautiful.

'He smiled and said "hi" to me, and I wanted to ask for a hug but the security guard forced me to just stand next to him and get the picture over with. He put his arm around my shoulder and I was freaking out inside! After the picture was taken, Justin turned to me and said, "You can stay if you want!" in his sexy voice – I think he said that because he saw that I was upset about the short time, and how the security guards treated me. I didn't get time to do anything because the security guard literally carried me out again. Afterwards, I decided to think positive and I started to realise how lucky I really was! I know that Justin cares about his fans no matter what, and he showed me that too and that was the sweetest thing. It was a night with a lot of emotions, but my dream came true that night.

'When I came into the concert I met Lisa, another security guard who works with Justin, and who was also at the Meet & Greet. I thought it was a nice chance to tell her about what I experienced with the other security guards. She was so supportive and nice to me, and said that she would talk about it to them – I hope that helped a little so they can treat fans a little nicer. The concert was totally amazing, words don't exist that can explain how fantastic it was. I had the perfect view and Justin was perfect as always. I really had the time of my life. I am so grateful for what I have experienced and I can't believe that I have been so close to the boy I love. I love Justin with all my heart and will always. I really hope I get the chance to see him again soon – I will never get enough of this boy!'

REBEKKA'S STORY

Rebekka is fifteen and from Oslo. Her favourite three songs are 'Love Me', 'Christmas Love' and 'Thought Of You'. She met Justin at the Sportpalaeis Arena in Antwerp, Belgium, with her friend Lilly. They also met guitarist Dan Kanter: 'We asked him about *Believe 3D* and he was like, "Yeah, Never Say Never... Ever!" He's so cute and very nice to the fans.' When she met Justin, she admits: 'I just stood there looking at his face. Like, you know in movies when they are saying, "It was like the whole room disappeared, the only thing I could see was him" – well, that was literally me right there. After only seeing him on a computer screen for so long, he seemed so big. His face was so beautiful. He looked like a real badass, it was unreal.'

Rebekka had a great time at the concert afterwards. 'The Believe Tour concert was the best! My friend and I had a huge Norwegian flag and we were holding it over the outside of the barrier (we had front row!) and Justin was looking and staring at us several times.

The audience was so loud and we had our incredible "special moment". It was amazing! I just want to say thank you to my friend Lilly, who's the reason for all of this because she was the one who found tickets in Belgium, and to my family for allowing me to go all the way to Belgium to meet Justin.'

CHAPTER 25

POLAND

In July 2012, Polish Beliebers made a moving video for Justin, in which they said: 'Come to Poland, we still BELIEVE!' They created a well-polished video that was like a trailer to a Justin movie. It had Justin running from his car, performing in arenas, singing in a recording studio… and ended with photos of individual fans holding up signs, saying 'Polish Beliebers'.

Justin's My World Tour didn't visit Poland but his Believe Tour did, with the singer performing in Łód on 25 March 2013. Justin is not always able to use a private jet to get from country to country; to get to Poland he had to travel by bus from Italy. He struggled with the length of the journey, tweeting: 'LONGEST BUS RIDE EVER. #19hours.'

A few hours later, director Alfredo Flores tweeted: 'Gets off bus *stretches* and yells WE FINALLY MADE IT!'

Justin wore his Canadian onesie as he checked out his hotel room – he was really impressed that it had its own library. He couldn't resist exploring the top shelves of the bookcases by climbing a big ladder and tweeted fans to ask: 'Anyone have a good book to recommend?'

After performing his Łód show, Justin didn't have much time to enjoy Poland as he was performing in Munich, Germany, three days later and so he had to fly out the next day. His visit might have been short but he still managed to meet lots of Polish Beliebers, who had been waiting for him outside his hotel, at the Meet & Greet and at the concert itself. As he left Poland through the security checkpoint at Wladyslaw Reymont Airport, fans managed to catch a glimpse of him without his shirt on.

The 'Justin Bieber Poland' Facebook page has over 30,000 fans and was set up in March 2011. Polish fans also have a Twitter account, which is worth following if you want to find out about the latest fan events – @BieberNewsPL.

CHAPTER 26

PORTUGAL

Portuguese Beliebers are very dedicated and, when they decided to hold a Bieber flash mob in January 2011, they had no idea it would end up on TV. The event was shown on the news and journalists interviewed some of the organisers to find out more. However, the flash mob was just one event that *JustinBieber-Portugal.com* have put on to show their hero just how much Portuguese Beliebers love him. The site is run by superfans Rita Duarte, Filipa Freire and Vivian Perez, with eight other Beliebers organising the fan events.

On 7 June 2012, Justin was interviewed by TVI Portugal and left his Portuguese fans a special message. He said: 'To all my Portuguese fans I love you so much and I'm going to come to Portugal really soon, I promise.'

Justin, his dancers and crew love visiting Portugal and performing for Portuguese fans. They didn't visit during the My World Tour but they did perform their Believe Tour concert on 11 March 2013 in Lisbon. Originally, there was to be a second show on 12 March but this was cancelled due to 'unforeseen circumstances'.

After Justin had performed in Lisbon, guitarist Dan Kanter tweeted: 'Wow! One of the craziest audiences we've played for! Thank you Lisbon for an unforgettable night!'

Justin tweeted: 'Thanks to all the fans...the beliebers tonight. incredible show!'

CHAPTER 27

RUSSIA

Justin loved visiting Russia in April 2013 to perform his Believe Tour concert on 28 April in St Petersburg and on 30 April in Moscow. He hadn't been able to visit the country as part of his My World Tour.

To welcome Justin to Russia, Beliebers held a flash mob in a shopping centre in St Petersburg. They wore purple tops and hats, and their dancing was very slick and polished. Having Justin come to Russia was very special because they had been campaigning for a long time. They had posted numerous videos on YouTube and one fan, Natty Frolova, had set up a petition on Twitter.

While in Moscow, Justin had time to play some ice

hockey with his friends, which was great fun. He also helped bodyguard Kenny Hamilton celebrate his birthday with a huge cake!

DID YOU KNOW?

Justin wrote one or two songs every day during his Believe Tour and kept them in a music journal. He made sure to write down the name of the city where he wrote each song too. Because he wrote over 200 songs, not all of them will be released but just the process of songwriting every day will help him become an even better artist.

CHAPTER 28

SOUTH AFRICA

In September 2010, Justin flew into South Africa for a short break before he had to head off to Hawaii to perform. He used the thirty-hour flight to catch up on some sleep, since he had been feeling rundown and tired before he got onto the plane. During his holiday, he went on an amazing safari at the Idube Game Reserve, seeing giraffes, rhinos, big cats and a huge crocodile. He took some photos, and a video was taken and posted on YouTube. To see it, search for 'Justin Bieber on a Safari in South Africa'.

Justin visited South Africa again in January 2011, posting a video of himself playing a cowbell with an African band and dancing. He wrote: 'I uploaded this on my twitvid too but this is me in S. Africa at this spot called Mama Africa in Cape Town. The band was playing and I decided to just jump up and join them. Everyone was staring at me at dinner so I just figured what the heck let's party!! It was great and me and the band had alot of fun. I LOVE MUSIC!! MAMA AFRICA!!'

Justin didn't perform his My World Tour concert in South Africa but he did perform his Believe Tour concert on 8 May 2013 in Cape Town and on 12 May 2013 in Johannesburg. Canadians celebrate Mother's Day on the second Sunday in May, which happened to be the day when Justin was performing in Johannesburg. He decided to surprise his mom by having her be his 'One Less Lonely Girl'. To see a video of what happened, search on YouTube for 'Justin Bieber – One Less Lonely Girl (Joburg) – Pattie OLLG'.

Justin also tweeted: 'Happy Mother's Day @pattiemallette. Today u r my #OLLG. Love u.'

Director Alfredo Flores tweeted: 'Happy Mother's Day @pattiemallette! You will forever be Justin's OLLG! Love u.'

During their time in South Africa, one of Justin's dancers posted a photo of fans watching the show and this message: 'Proud of our dancers, band, crew & boss @justinbieber! But, none of this would be possible without our #beliebers! We love you!

'Took this photo tonight during "Believe". Memories brought me back to the question that changed my life – "Why do you want to be a part of the Believe tour?!" My answer then was that I wanted to be a part of something inspirational, a journey created by the power of belief. In yourself, your talents, and every single dream you've ever dreamt. My answer still stands, and after almost 100 shows I'm proud to say that my dreams became my reality. I have left my heart on each stage all around the world, and have been inspired by beautiful people who share the same thing – a dream. ANYTHING is possible, if you believe. #BelieveTour.'

If you want to follow the dancer on Twitter, her Twitter name is @carlenabritch.

Justin really enjoyed his dates in South Africa and going to places he'd never visited before. On 8 May, he explored Cape Town on his bike at night. He didn't get hassled as he might have done, had he attempted the same trip in the daytime.

CHAPTER 29

SPAIN

In November 2010, Justin visited Spain and he was presented with a plaque for *My Worlds: The Collection* going Gold. The presentation took place at the Urban Hotel in Madrid. Justin loves receiving different commemorative plaques from the different countries he visits because each one is special, as they show how much support his Beliebers in that particular country have given him by buying his albums.

Justin performed his My World Tour concert in Spain on 5 April 2011 in Madrid and 6 April 2011 in Barcelona. During the Barcelona concert, he performed the Spanish dance song 'La Macarena', which was a worldwide hit in 1995/6. Justin visited Spain again in November 2011 while promoting his

Christmas album, and in June 2012 to promote his album *Believe*. For the June trip, he was joined by his dad, Jeremy, and his sister, Jazzy.

Justin performed his Believe Tour concert on 14 March 2013 in Madrid and 16 March 2013 in Barcelona. After his Believe show at the Palacio de los Deportes stadium in Madrid, he tweeted: 'MADRID!! Gracias! Thank u!! great show! now on to Barcelona! #BelieveTour.'

So many fans turned up to see Justin wherever he went in Spain that his security team had to be very vigilant to make sure that he wasn't put in any risky situations.

When Justin visited Spain, he was fortunate enough to be invited to train with the Barcelona football team. His friend Ryan Butler was with him and so the two of them had a blast kicking a ball around with some of the best footballers in the world. On Barcelona's website, there was a news report about the visit and they wrote that Justin had 'surprisingly decent skills with his left foot'.

Beliebers weren't surprised to learn that Justin had impressed the people at Barcelona because he is very sporty and likes playing football/soccer with his friends. He is a football fan and, when Spain won the World Cup final, beating the Netherlands 1–0, he tweeted: 'Wow...SPAIN!! great game...nothing to be ashamed of. True champions on both sides. Congrats to Spain.'

DID YOU KNOW?

When Justin wants to send a girl some flowers, he picks sunflowers because they are his favourite flower.

Spanish Beliebers have their own website – *www.JustinBieberSpainFans.org* – and the Justin Bieber Spain Facebook page has over 160,000 fans.

KAROLINA'S STORY

Karolina is fourteen and from Madrid. Her favourite songs are 'One Less Lonely Girl', 'Stuck In The Moment' and 'Yellow Raincoat'. She says: 'Being a Belieber here in Spain is quite difficult because people don't like Justin and judge you really hard for it. It's quite challenging to find another Belieber because they're very rare and most of the Beliebers keep their love for Justin a secret. He doesn't come very often and, when he does, he stays for a short time.'

Karolina became a Belieber in 2009. As she explains: 'My father died, and Justin was just starting out as an artist. I was so depressed. One day

I went to sleep over at my friend's house and she started showing me videos of Justin on YouTube. Long story short, Justin got me out of my depression with his amazing voice, down-to-earth personality and great looks, of course.

'On April 5th 2011, Justin had a show in Palacio de los Deportes in Madrid. He was supposed to be staying in the Urban Hotel, but he actually stayed in a little town 45 minutes away. I didn't know this, though, so me and my mom rented a room at the Urban Hotel and we stayed in the lobby for fifteen and a half hours waiting for him. I was so disappointed that I didn't get to see him. The next day was the show and I met [guitarist] Dan Kanter. I gave him a letter to give to Justin, explaining that I had been waiting to see him the day before. I don't know if he passed it on, but I also gave it to a man from the radio station and faxed it to his REAL hotel too.

'The date I actually got to meet Justin for the first time was November 11th 2011. Justin had an interview on the *El Hormiguero* TV show at 6pm. I was waiting in a little room next to the door he was supposed to come in through. When he arrived, I poked my head out the door and said, "Justin, wait," but I didn't move, and then another security guard (not Kenny [Hamilton], a mean one) screamed at me and told me to back off. I went back into the little room and cried my eyes out. Later, before the show ended, I was going to the bathroom to fix my hair and I saw Scrappy. He asked me where the toilets were, so I told him and he thanked me. Then, fifteen minutes later, I was on a staircase waiting for Justin and I heard him singing. I went up the stairs and said, "Justin, wait!" but he probably didn't hear me so my mom screamed, "JUSTIN, WAIT, SHE JUST WANTS TO GIVE YOU SOMETHING, IT'S ONE SECOND!" and he heard (it's hard not to hear my mom, LOLZ).

'He stopped and was like, "Yeah?" and I went up to him and I said "Hi' very softly. I gave him a white baseball cap that said "Madrid" on it and he smiled and said, "Oh, thank you." My mom was looking for her camera and Justin kept saying, "Picture, picture, you wanna take a picture?" and pretended that he had a camera, clicking the invisible button. He waited and my mom finally found the camera, but a security woman said [in Spanish]: "Times up, he has to go – no pictures, times up!" She grabbed Justin by his arm and tried blocking him so that he couldn't get close to me. He told her, "No, why don't YOU wait a minute? Stop!" and the lady backed off and he smiled and took a picture with me.

'Once Justin left, I started shaking and my knees went weak and I fell to the floor, bawling because my dream had just come true. Then I saw Alfredo Flores and he was like, "What's wrong? Are you okay?" – I was crying so hard. I said, "I just met Justin Bieber!" and he told me, "That's so great!!" and gave me a BIG hug and a kiss on the head. I took a picture with him and I told him, "Please make sure Justin gets my letter." He said, "Don't worry, I got you!" and left.'

NÚRIA'S STORY

Núria is sixteen and from Barcelona. Her favourite three songs are 'Be Alright', 'That Should Be Me' and 'Nothing Like Us'. Núria has visited Stratford and she met Justin when he performed in Barcelona. She takes up her story: 'July 14th 2012 is a day I will never forget – it was the day I went to Stratford. You may be thinking, "What? A Spanish Belieber in Stratford?" But yeah, I WENT TO STRATFORD. I was studying English in Canada for a month and staying with an amazing host family, who made one of my dreams come true. They live an hour and a half away from there and I spent the whole journey singing along to Justin's song with them and my friend Belén. I was crying and sobbing when I got there. For someone who's from a small town near Barcelona, Spain, it was something that seemed an impossible dream. It was one of the best days of my life. I sat on the steps of the Avon Theatre, where it all started. Unbelievable!

'My biggest dream came true, after almost five years of being a Belieber, when I finally met Justin Drew Bieber Mallette. It all started on 18 December 2012. I had floor tickets to go to Justin's concert in Barcelona on 16 March 2013, but that day my friend sent me a link that said that they were selling Meet & Greet. I cried for almost an hour trying to convince my mum to buy them and told her that I'd give her the money if she did it. I was so scared they would be sold out by the time my mum said yes, but luckily they weren't so I bought one.

'I decided to give my other ticket to a Belieber who couldn't afford to buy one. It's all about giving back, right? From that moment, I knew that I had to do something for other Beliebers who didn't have the opportunity to meet Justin, so I made a professional scrapbook for him. I spent hours and hours working on it and it cost me almost €300. I was hoping Justin or someone from the team would see it.

'On March 16, 2013, I got up really early because of my nerves. I prepared everything for the concert and the Meet & Greet and at 11 o'clock we (my mum, my dad, my neighbour's sister and I) left for Justin's hotel in Barcelona, Hotel Arts. We waited there for about an hour and a half, but Justin didn't come out and I had to go to the venue so I couldn't stay any longer. Hours passed really, really, really slow but then it was 4.30pm and I knew I had to be in the line for the Meet & Greet at 4.45pm. A lady came to talk to us and explained what we could and couldn't do at the Meet & Greet.

'We finally got inside the room where we were gonna meet Justin, and there was this black curtain, which we knew would have Justin stood at the other side. How can I explain my feelings right in that moment? There were two lines – the ones who had bought the tickets and the ones who had won them. I was so nervous, the people who were standing next to me in the line were flipping out. That was funny, though. I had the scrapbooks in my hands – yes, two – and the other gifts for him: a necklace that says "Make it about the music" and some letters from other Beliebers. I then saw Kenny [Hamilton] and Alfredo [Flores]. They came out of the curtain room and we could all catch a glimpse of Justin. HE WAS PERFECT! The Meet & Greet started and it was all so fast – you didn't get to talk to him, or that's what it seemed like.

'I was the last one with an individual picture. Kenny saw me and came to me so I could get inside before the group ones. I showed him the scrapbooks and he promised me he'd make Justin read them. Kenny was so nice and he told me I was so cute and to have fun. Then he opened the curtain and the first thing I saw was Alfredo. Then I turned to my right to face Justin. HE IS INCREDIBLY HANDSOME.

'He was wearing black jeans, a white T-shirt, a black jacket and sunglasses. I was trying to go to Justin but I was in so much shock that I couldn't move. Alfredo was kind of laughing about the situation. Justin looked at me – I couldn't really tell if he was checking me out or he was staring at my clothes or something. Alfredo looked at me, looked at Justin and then Justin looked at me and he said, "Come here," with a cute and soft voice. I managed to walk up to him and he came at me and gave me the biggest and sweetest hug ever. He was so sweet the whole time. He didn't have to, though – I'm already in love with him.

'While in his arms, I said, "Hi, Justin." He replied to me with, "Hi, sweetie, how are you?" I don't know how but it seemed like a conversation between two friends who hadn't seen each other for a long time. I said, "Good, I couldn't be better," and he pulled away from the hug slowly and giggled. He had a smile on his face the whole time. "Good, perfect." He grabbed my hand while saying that and turned me around. We were both facing the camera and, before I could even prepare myself, I heard him say, "SMILE!" I swear he took one of the best pictures of all the Meet & Greets. He looks so silly, just how we love to see him. After we took the picture, I said, "Thank you so much, Justin," and, of course, he's such a flirt, he has to kill me with his words. He said, "No, thank YOU, sweetie." I was in shock; I didn't even know what I was doing. I told him, "I love you," and he said, "I love you too." He hugged me again.

'The bodyguard who was controlling the Meet & Greet came to me and grabbed my shoulders, trying to push me away from Justin. But Justin was hugging me even tighter. I tried to say, "I love you" again but words didn't come out from my mouth. Justin understood me perfectly, though. He said, "Te amo" with a sexy, raspy voice. Oh my gosh, that was perfect! It was the last thing we said to each other because the bodyguard wanted me to leave.

'I swear Justin was looking at me with an "I'm so sorry" face and that broke my heart for a second. I was walking out and turned to see Justin again. He was smiling at me, winked at me and blew me a kiss to say goodbye.'

CHAPTER 30

SWEDEN

In December 2011, Swedish Beliebers organised a demonstration in the centre of Stockholm in front of the Canadian Embassy to show Justin just how much he means to them. Thousands of fans took part, singing Justin's songs and holding up banners asking him to come to Sweden. Justin was really touched when he heard what they had done – he is so grateful to every single person who supports him.

Justin didn't perform his My World Tour concert in Sweden but he did perform three Believe Tour concerts in Stockholm on 22, 23 and 24 April 2013. When he arrived in the country, he wore a strange

Chanel mask and hat so that only his eyes and mouth were showing.

DID YOU KNOW?

After his final show, Justin went clubbing with DJ Tay James, even though both of them must have been tired.

When Justin was staying at the Grand Hotel in Stockholm, some pranksters decided to have fun at the cost of the fans waiting outside. They hired a limousine and one of them dressed up to look like Justin. The fake bodyguard held a jacket over the fake Justin's face as he got out of the car and ran into the hotel. Everyone started screaming because they thought it was the real Justin. Five minutes later, the pranksters got back in their limousine and drove off, waving to fans who genuinely thought it must be Justin. The local police had to hold back Beliebers who surrounded the car and tried to chase it as it drove away.

When the real Justin was in Stockholm, he wore a red onesie and performed with rapper Lil Za as he walked to his tour bus. He didn't hide his face and waved to fans; he was also spotted with a new tiger tattoo on his arm.

In a 2012 interview with Swedish TV channel TV4, Justin was asked what family mean to him. He replied: 'Family in general, you know, it means the world to me, you know. I was always an only child then recently in the last couple of years I was blessed enough to have a little brother and sister, who now I get to see and they come to see me in LA and stuff. It's been really cool.

'I took them to Disney World for the first time, which was awesome.'

DID YOU KNOW?

One of the most common questions that fans want to ask Justin is 'Will you marry me?'

ISABELLE'S STORY

Thirteen-year-old Isabelle is from Stockholm. Her favourite three songs are 'Down To Earth', 'Never Let You Go' and 'Mistletoe'. On Justin's nineteenth birthday, Isabelle took part in a flash mob but it was ruined by haters who turned up and attacked the fans (thankfully, no one was seriously hurt). It was horrible but hasn't discouraged her from attending future fan events.

She met Justin at a Meet & Greet at the Globe

arena in Stockholm. She says: 'Once we got inside, I was surprised. The "Meet & Greet Room" was just a big hall, with grey curtains and a black, ugly carpeted floor. The only thing in there was some red chairs in a line. After a couple of minutes, Ryan came in. Ryan is Justin's bodyguard, or "The Host", and he told us all the rules for our meeting: we had to ask Justin for a hug before we hugged him, we had to leave our gifts on a table outside the Meet & Greet tent, we couldn't ask for an autograph, we couldn't kiss him... stuff like that.

'We sat in the room for about two hours. Suddenly, Ryan said, "Everybody, go to your seats." We all did as he said, and suddenly Dan [Kanter] came out. I almost fainted. I watched him wide-eyed while he stood and talked to Ryan. Suddenly a tall blonde girl from the back row walked up to him and started to talk to Dan, even though Ryan had said that we couldn't get up. But it looked like Dan knew her, because he gave her a hug. When Dan left, I started to cry, and it made me worried. All I could think was, "If I cry when I see Dan, how will I react when I meet Justin Bieber himself?"

'When I was done crying, I went to the toilets and fixed my make-up and then walked to Ryan. He was stood talking to some girls. I stuttered, "Uhm... Ryan... Can-can... I-I-I Please have a h-hug?" and he smiled at me and laughed a little and then said, "Yeah, of course," and I literally threw myself on him and hugged him really tight, and started to cry hysterically again.

'After a while, Ryan told us, "Everybody, go to the Meet & Greet line," and, just as we were about to take our place in the line, Justin came on his Segway! And he said something like "Hey, everybody!" and drove back to the Meet & Greet tent. Me? Oh, I was in shock – I just stood there and stared after him. When it was my turn, a security guard pushed me and some of the others inside the tent and I put on a Justin mask that I borrowed from my friend Cassandra. Justin looked at me and laughed. I made him laugh! Then I took the mask off right before Justin said, "Hey there, sweetheart." Before I could answer, he pulled me in for a soft and warm hug. I didn't even ask for the hug, he just hugged me! It felt like I was going to die. Before I took my place on Justin's right side, I said quickly, "Hey, Justin, can we please do funny faces on the picture?" Justin nodded and laughed as he said, "Yeah, of course, sweetie."

'He then took the Justin mask and placed it in front of his face, and the guy took two pictures of us. After that, the security guard started to drag me away from him so I started to walk away. All of a sudden, I felt someone's hand around my wrist and I turned around. And guess who it was? Justin! Justin pulled me in another warm and long hug. He said, "Don't go, just one more picture, please?" I couldn't believe it – Justin Drew Bieber wanted more pictures with ME!

'When Justin hugged me, I placed my cheek against his chest and his chin rested on top of my head. I said, "I love you so much, Justin," and he got all shy and embarrassed, and he smiled with his eyes closed as he said, "I love you too."'

HARLEE'S STORY

Fifteen-year-old Harlee is from Stockholm. Her favourite three songs are 'As Long As You Love Me', 'Love Me Like You Do' and 'Favorite Girl'. She says: 'Being a Swedish Belieber is really great except the fact that Justin barely comes here because we are so far away. He has only been here once but, apart from that, everyone supports each other!

'I found out Justin was coming to Sweden last summer and I totally freaked out. A couple of months before the concert, the ticket site announced they were releasing more Meet & Greet tickets. The same hour I found out about it, my mom drove me to outside the ticket place where they would be selling them the next day. There were five girls in the queue already. My mom got us some food, a sleeping bag, blankets, etc. because we were going to sleep outside. The next day at about 12pm, the people who sold the tickets came out and told us we had to wait many more hours for the tickets. It was hard waiting, but the second I had my ticket in my hand, I was so happy and excited.

'Sooner than I expected, the big day arrived and I was about to meet Justin. Once again, I was all by myself and lined up outside the backstage area. I showed my ticket, and got a wristband. While waiting for Justin, Dan [Kanter] came – and a dancer. The VIP host Ryan came and he was really funny; he told us that Justin was there and everyone freaked out. When we got in line to go into the little room with curtains, Justin came out on his Segway, waved and said, "Hey, everybody!" before he rauhled into the tent again (see what I did there!).

'It all went pretty fast from there and, finally, it was my turn. When I saw Justin in front of me I just wanted to cry, but I couldn't. I looked up at him and said, "Justin, can you please smile?" and he looked into my eyes and smiled the biggest smile with this little giggle. It was the cutest thing I've ever seen. Then he placed one arm around me and placed me beside him. The photos were taken and he grabbed my hand quickly before I went outside. I still couldn't cry – it was the best few seconds of my life. Thank you, Justin Drew Bieber, for making my biggest dream come true.'

CHAPTER 31

SWITZERLAND

In July 2011, Swiss Beliebers gathered in Zürich to sing and dance together. Many of the fans wore Justin's favourite colour: purple. There have been lots of meet-ups and events since then as Swiss Beliebers love hanging out together.

Justin performed his My World Tour concert in Zürich on 8 April 2011. Before the show, he tweeted: 'Zurich switzerland...and a fan has already brought me a swiss army knife. im ready. #myworldtour.'

Sadly for Justin, he didn't have much time to explore during his trip because, as soon as he finished his concert, he had to leave as he was performing in Milan, Italy, the very next night.

In an interview with *SF* in Zurich, Justin was

asked about his fans. He said: 'I think my fans are amazing – they've been amazing since day one. I think that it's great that I am able to have such a close relationship with them over the internet. Having Twitter and Facebook and being able to, you know, interact with them, I think that's what makes a big difference between, say, this day and age and, like, twenty years ago because they didn't even have Twitter, they didn't have anything to really interact with their fans. And now the fans feel like they're really part of me and it's important.'

Justin performed his Believe Tour concert on 22 March 2013. During his visit, he stayed at the Dolder Grand Hotel in Zurich. He couldn't resist coming out onto the balcony and waving at fans down below. He also spent time on the Alps, tweeting a couple of photos of himself and his crew with snowboards, and told fans: 'Snowboarding this morning and working this afternoon. We go hard fun day in the Alps so far.'

DID YOU KNOW?

Justin sleeps on his side and on his stomach. He likes to have one pillow rather than two.

While in Zurich, Justin's bus was surrounded by so many Swiss Beliebers that he couldn't help but capture it on video. He later posted up the video so fans could see for themselves, tweeting: 'I was taking a look at my phone and found this old video of Zurich. Grateful Beliebers.'

In the recording, Justin says: 'They will not let us leave. Look at this, this is our bus. We are now surrounded. And they just do not let us leave! What do we do, Mike?'

CHAPTER 32

TURKEY

In June 2012, Turkish fans campaigned for Justin to visit their country by doing a parade in Taksim in Istanbul. They carried banners saying 'I have Bieber Fever', 'I love J Biebs' and chanted his name. There are several Turkish pages for Justin on Facebook, one of the most popular being 'Justin Bieber Turkey Fun Club', which has over 30,000 fans.

Justin didn't visit Turkey on his My World Tour but he did perform his Believe Tour concert there on 2 May 2013 in Istanbul. It was an open-air concert rather than being in an enclosed arena, unlike the majority of his other shows.

Justin is very popular in Turkey and, when he arrived in the country by private plane at Istanbul's

Sabiha Gökçen Airport, he was greeted by lots of excited Beliebers. For safety reasons, he had to jump straight into a car as soon as he got off the plane and had his passport checked afterwards. He tweeted: 'Turkey is crazy right now. We ready.'

When Justin was performing his Believe concert in Istanbul, he showed great respect by pausing twice during the event to honour the Azan. The Azan is the Islamic Call to Prayer and happens five times every day. Fans in the arena tweeted about how much they admired Justin for doing so because it would have been easy for him not to.

During his time in the country, he was interviewed by *Gulf News*, who asked what romantic things he likes to do. He replied: 'I think that the most romantic things to do for someone are the things that you spend time on – like, having a picnic where you bring all the stuff they like. You make it something that she's going to remember so she can tell all of her friends. Stuff she can say, "He did this for me!" That's great.

'I think it's up to the guy to be romantic. I think it's the guy's responsibility to take her out – it can't be the other way around. That would take away my masculinity, I feel if that would happen.'

> ### DID YOU KNOW?
>
> For a video for the Believe Tour, Justin had to get into a shark tank and he really didn't like it because he is scared of sharks. It took him an hour to pluck up the courage to jump in. He found that it helped having members of the Aqualillies Synchronized Swimming Troupe around him, because the girls kept the sharks and stingrays at a distance. When Justin holidayed in the Bahamas in August 2013, he saw some nurse sharks in the wild. He was at the Staniel Cay Yacht Club with his friends Ryan Butler and Lil Za at the time. Justin decided to get in the water with them and go for a swim.

ECE'S STORY

Sixteen-year-old Ece is from Ankara, the capital of Turkey. Her favourite three songs are 'One Time', 'Fall' and 'Believe'. She became a Belieber in 2010 and met Justin in Istanbul on 2 May 2013. Ece also met Justin's dancers and DJ Tay James at their hotel. She says: 'I saw Justin's foot first – he was wearing red Supra and dark trousers. When I saw his face, I was speechless – it was more beautiful than in videos and photos. It was like he wasn't real: his face was flawless, the whole of him was flawless. I asked him, "Can you hug me?" – I didn't want to miss the opportunity. He said, "Yeah," and smiled.

'I'd been waiting for a hug from him for three years – it was magical!'

DAPHNE'S STORY

Daphne is sixteen and also from Ankara. Her favourite three songs are 'Down To Earth', 'Never Let You Go' and 'Nothing Like Us'. She always defends Justin if she hears people saying nasty things about him. Daphne has been a Belieber since 2010 and met Justin on 2 May 2013. She takes up her story: 'When they announced that Justin was coming to Turkey, I lost it. The tickets were finally out. My mom, my cousins, my aunt, myself, everyone was trying to buy me tickets for the front row. The site said, "Sold Out" and I couldn't believe it. I started crying like crazy. I started praying to God, "God, please let me have tickets, please, please." Then my cousin said, "DAPHNE, THE TICKETS ARE BACK ON!" I was so shocked and happy when we managed to get some.

'On 2 May, me, my best friend and my mom went to Istanbul. We found Justin's hotel and went there. People said we had just missed Justin, and that he had just gone inside. We knew that Justin would be sleeping so we left because the next day was the concert and I would be meeting him then, anyway. We went to the arena and finally got in the area for VIPs. We were told all the rules that were and weren't allowed when meeting Justin. We started waiting for them to let us in. My mom called me and told me she met Kenny [Hamilton] and Dan [Kanter]! I was pretty jealous but also amused by the fact that my mom knew who Kenny and Dan were, and that made me happy.

'Finally, they started letting us in. There were five people ahead of me and Justin was in a tent, taking pictures. I looked inside the tent – it was really dark and I couldn't see anything. Then a flash popped out of nowhere and lit up Justin's face. I was shocked, I really was – I couldn't believe he was right in front of me. My brain was like, "OFDKMGNDJFGHUDGJ" but, on the outside, I tried to act cool. When there were two girls ahead of me, Justin looked right at me: he was staring at me and I was staring at him. We looked at each other for five seconds and then he turned to his bodyguard and then looked away. His bodyguard looked at me and pointed at me, saying, "Come in." I started shaking. Justin Bieber was in front of me, he wasn't some picture on my computer; he was actually there.

'"Hi, Justin, I love you so much," I said very quickly, still in shock. He said, "I love you too," and

I collapsed inside. "Can I have a hug?" I was trying so hard not to cry. He said, "Of course," in a cute way. His skin was flawless. I hugged him really tight. He wrapped one arm over my shoulder and he held my arm with his other hand. I was still hugging him so he turned me around and made me face the camera but he didn't let go of me. I smiled at the camera. After the picture was taken, I had to go. I held his hand and said, "I love you so much – you changed my life." He smiled at me, which melted my heart, and thanked me.

'That was it – I met the love of my life; I met the boy who saved my life. When I went out of the tent, I burst into tears. I started sobbing so bad. Some people came up to me and asked me if I was okay. I was more than okay, I was floating in air; I was on Cloud 9! Justin Bieber told me he loved me! What? Then the concert started. I was really close to the stage. It was the best day of my sixteen years of existence – I lost my voice but it was totally worth it.'

CHAPTER 33

UNITED ARAB EMIRATES

Justin didn't perform his My World Tour concert in the United Arab Emirates but he did perform his Believe Tour concert on 4 and 5 May 2013 in Dubai. Originally, he had planned to perform only one show but, when his show in Oman was cancelled, he decided to do an extra date in Dubai. Newspapers reported that the show had been cancelled because Justin's dance routines were deemed too sexy.

During his stay in the city, he drove a white Lamborghini Aventador to the arena. He also went clubbing with Lil Twist and spent time on the beach. He tweeted: 'Just chillin with the fellas in Dubai. no big deal. haha.'

Poor Justin had a fright during his performance of

'Believe' when a man managed to get onstage and went to hug him. He was at his piano at the time, but the man was quickly tackled by security. The piano ended up being knocked over but Justin carried on singing, moving to the other side of the stage until the intruder was taken away. Fans in the audience were so shocked because the man could have had a weapon and because it all happened so fast. To see a video of what happened, search for 'Justin Bieber incident in Dubai concert' on YouTube.

Justin obviously doesn't like fans that take things to the extreme as the man did, but he adores his other Beliebers. He told *ET*: 'I love my fans. I love the way they interact with me – how they're just so happy. I just love it.

'I'm never going to get over that – I never want to lose my young fans.'

CHAPTER 34

UK

Justin has a huge fan base in the UK. His UK Beliebers arranged a Bieber Parade in London on 25 October 2010 to encourage him to visit them again and to show how much he means to them. He had been over in June 2010 for Capital FM's Summertime Ball concert, but they wanted to see him again. The parade was organised by superfans Hasti and Gulcan, with 200 Beliebers taking part. Three weeks after the London parade, UK Beliebers were delighted to learn that Justin's My World Tour was coming to the UK. He was to play ten dates around the UK. His first stop was Birmingham on 4 and 5 March (then he was going to Dublin, Ireland for a show on 8th), then Liverpool (11th),

Newcastle (12th), London (14th, 16th and 17th), Manchester (20th), Sheffield (23rd) and ending in Nottingham (24th).

Justin visited the UK again in 2012 to promote his *Believe* album. When his Believe Tour dates were announced, UK Beliebers were as pleased as they had been when the My World Tour dates were announced: from 21 February to 8 March 2013, he would be performing ten shows again.

DID YOU KNOW?

While visiting London, Justin went to Buckingham Palace with guitarist Dan Kanter and did some busking outside. He didn't collect any money, but just sang some of his songs to the tourists. The people watching couldn't believe that Justin Bieber was there in front of them!

When interviewed by Aled Jones on TV show *Daybreak*, Justin was asked if UK fans are different from American fans. He replied: 'A little bit. In the States, they chase the car for a little bit, but here they chase the car and run from block to block, then grab their bikes! They're very dedicated.

'I never get fed up with it. So many people wish to

have the fan base that I have, so I don't get fed up with anything.'

He also admitted that he misses his mom when she isn't with him, saying: 'I do miss her now I'm eighteen. Before she was around all the time and I would get sick of her and I would look forward to her leaving. I'd be like, "Yes! Mom's leaving tomorrow!" Now I'm like, "When's Mom coming back?"'

'It's funny how things change.'

During Justin's promotional tour of the UK in September 2012, he started to feel ill. He had been working non-stop promoting his biography, *Justin Bieber: Just Getting Started*, and his *Believe* album around the world. On 12 September, he tweeted fans: 'Sick and frustrated. #beingsicksucks.'

Five days later, he said: 'All the travel and the body finally broke down. Soo sick. Just gonna chill. No fun.'

Fans decided that they would try to cheer Justin up by sticking Post-it notes to the window of his car so that he could read their 'get well soon' messages as he travelled from place to place. Justin was really touched and, after taking some photos of the messages, he wrote: 'This is why I love u. When I'm sick u cheer me up thanks for the nice words.

'I love my beliebers. Thanks for making me feel better.'

DID YOU KNOW?

When Justin performed in Liverpool on 11 March, 500 fans turned up at his hotel, resulting in the surrounding roads being closed. He was ordered to stay in his hotel by the police for his own safety. However, he did manage to make one trip to Alder Hey Children's Hospital, which was really important to him because he wanted to make the children on the cancer ward smile. A spokesperson from the hospital told the BBC: 'When people like Justin Bieber take the time to come and visit our patients it gives them a tremendous boost and really cheers everyone up.

'Patients on the oncology ward undergo rigorous treatments and you can actually see in the children what a difference it makes to have a visitor they admire from the world of entertainment or sport.'

DID YOU KNOW?

Justin might love visiting the UK but he could never move there permanently, as he explained to Fearne Cotton on BBC Radio 1: 'I couldn't live here because the weather's depressing. Very depressing. But I like the girls!'

While in London performing his Believe show at the O2 Arena on 7 March 2013, Justin didn't feel very well and he was struggling to breathe. He insisted on carrying on with the show, though, because he didn't want to let his Beliebers down. Afterwards, he collapsed backstage and was taken to hospital to get checked out. To make matters worse, the next day the paparazzi were waiting for him outside his hotel and Justin lost his temper. But it wasn't his fault: after all, he'd had hardly any sleep and wasn't feeling himself. He tweeted afterwards: 'Ahhhhh! Rough morning. Trying to feel better for this show tonight but let the paps get the best of me... Sometimes when people r shoving cameras in your face all day and yelling the worst thing possible at u...well I'm human. Rough week.

'Not gonna let them get the best of me again. Gonna get focused on this show tonight. Adrenaline is high now. Gonna put it on the stage.'

Manager Scooter Braun cannot understand why the UK press is so negative about Justin. While outside Justin's hotel, he was approached by a journalist who mistakenly thought he was the dad of a fan.

Scooter explained via Twitter what happened: 'Learned alot about the press over here tonight. when i arrived back at my hotel i was approached by someone who thought i was a parent... they said can we film u for the news about Justin Bieber and can u say how angry u are at him and would i mind saying i hate him....

'...fans then ran over and said this had been commonplace all day. U should have seen the face when they found out i was his manager... bottom line is people who focus on negative things end with negative results. We will focus on the positive and feel bad for those that cant.

'i have seen some crazy things the last couple of years but today was pretty wild. lol. Gonna keep it moving.

'and for the press..i know u think u need to make up negative things to sell papers... but if u had a little more faith in the public u would see WE all want to hear the positive things in life. Have some faith in humanity!'

Justin was equally upset as the press really criticised him that week, saying he had been two hours late for one of the concerts and writing as many negative stories about him as possible. He tweeted to set the record straight and to let fans know how he was feeling: 'Rumors rumors and more rumors. nothing more nothing less. might talk about them 1 day. rt now im just gonna be positive. cant bring me down.

'im focused on the good things in life. im blessed and not forgetting it. im giving back every day for it. cant phase me.

'fake stories to sell papers i guess are part of the job. but im a good person. i know that. u cant tell me different. we know the truth .. as long as my family, friends, and fans r with me u can say whatever. we are all equal in God's eyes & we have a responsibility to each other.'

It was really hard for Justin because it should have been a week to celebrate turning nineteen. He managed to enjoy a nice Indian meal with his friends and crew at Mint Leaf Restaurant, but when they went to a club they got lots of hassle from the paparazzi and the club's security so they left. Justin had paid $15,000 (over £9,000) to hold a circus-themed party in the club, but because not all of his guests were over eighteen they couldn't come in and he didn't want to have the party without them. He tweeted that it was his worst birthday ever, but later said he didn't mean it because he still enjoyed being with those friends who had flown over specially. The thing he didn't like was how aggressive people were to him and his team and the fact that some Beliebers were knocked over by the press.

Justin got lots of tweets from his celebrity friends, who all wanted to wish him a happy birthday (and one from his mom too):

Carly Rae Jepsen: 'Happy Birthday to an incredible artist and friend. @JustinBieber ~enjoy 19!'

Cody Simpson: 'Happy birthday to my mate @justinbieber see u tonight.'

Miley Cyrus: 'I'm with every other @justinbieber fan. I wanna be at his birthday party! Shit gonnnnnna goooooo offffffffff! #turnup #19.'

Nicki Minaj: 'Happy Birthday my G!!! @justinbieber ;p'

Niall Horan: 'Big happy birthday @justinbieber, have a good day bro!'

Pattie Mallette: 'Happy 19th Birthday @justinbieber!! First Bday I'm not with you! Miss u like crazy. Have a good one!!! Love mom. Xoxo.'

DID YOU KNOW?

Justin's dad Jeremy bought his son an amazing nineteenth birthday present – a customised 'Bat Bike' MV Agusta motorbike. Jeremy couldn't come over to London so instead posted a video on YouTube to show Justin his present and explain its unique features. It has 35 mil. followers on the petrol tank (the number of followers Justin had on Twitter at the time), some of Justin's tattoos, a JB logo and the number 6, which was Justin's hockey number. At the end of the video, Jaxon and Jazmyn appear and wish their brother a happy birthday. Check out the video on YouTube by searching for 'Happy 19th Birthday Justin Bieber'.

SOPHIA'S STORY

Sophia is fifteen and from Doncaster. Her favourite three songs are 'Believe', 'That Should Be Me' and 'Nothing Like Us'. She says: 'I love Justin because I've grown up with him and watched him from the start, from nothing to being as successful as he is now. He does so much for charity, he's such an inspiration... his music has helped me through a lot. I only have one friend, Vanessa, from Doncaster, who loves Justin as much as me but I have lots of Belieber friends in London, Manchester and Sheffield. We all went to Birmingham and did a Bieber Parade to raise money for Justin's charity, Pencils of Promise, and it was such good fun!

'Here is my story of how I met Justin. For the last three to four years, my mum and I were prime carers for my granddad who lived with us. He had many illnesses, including heart failure, COPD, kidney disease, diabetes and arthritis. He had no use of his legs and was bedridden in the front room of our house. Despite all the pain he was going through, he always tried to put on a brave face. I always used to go into his room to watch Justin on award shows, music channels, and *Never Say Never* with him. He always used to shout to me when Justin was on the TV. He always used to say, "JUSTIN BEAVER IS ON!" but, when he actually watched *Never Say Never*, he had a lot of respect for Justin and could understand why thousands of girls admired him so much. Because I was always helping my mum with my granddad, he said to my mum, "Could we enter Sophia to one of those shows where dreams come true to meet Justin because I know how much he means to her and it's a thank you from me for her help?"

'My mum attempted to write a letter to the *Daybreak* TV show but didn't know what to do, so never sent it. She entered me in many competitions to meet Justin, but I didn't have a clue. One day the doctor told us he [Granddad] was dying and only had a few weeks left to live. He gave us the option for him to be in hospital or be at home. We said for him to stay home as there was nothing the hospital could do that we couldn't. From that day, the next two weeks were horrendous. Three to four times a day he was having hypos (low blood sugars) and it was a battle to even get him to drink, he wasn't eating and was only on fluids. In these two weeks, I was still going to school, trying to act like everything was okay but inside it was killing me. My best friend Tamara was helping us in the morning as it just got too hard for me and my mum to do it ourselves.

'My mum found out Justin was coming to the UK on 23 April, so my mum spoke to the school and explained the situation and asked for permission for me to have a small break to recharge, as it was too stressful for me. The school said it was fine and authorised my absence at school. So here it begins... My friend Amy and I went to London on 23 April. Originally we thought we were staying at a friend's house but, due to an illness in her family, we were unable to stay. As Amy was only seventeen we were unable to get a hotel because you had to be over eighteen. We decided – well, really had no option but to just stay outside Justin's hotel for the night. No blankets, no shelter, nothing; just the hope of seeing Justin. When I first got to Justin's hotel, I felt so excited yet anxious to what was going to happen.

'At about 1am on the Tuesday morning, Scooter [Braun] came out and told us to go home and get warm, and he promised us we would meet Justin. But we had nowhere to go so we just circled the area. At about 9am, there were about 20–30 people outside his hotel. I knew I wasn't going to get a photo but I still had the chance to see him. We saw a car at the bottom of the hotel drive and four girls were crowding it. Amy and I ran to the car and it was Justin. It felt like my heart fell to my stomach, I was in complete shock. My eyes lit up and all I could say was, "I love you, Justin." He held my hand through the car window and said, "I love you too." I didn't know what to do with myself, he was looking right at me. He then drove off and we found out he was at KISS FM. We decided to go there too.

'Justin came out and there were paps EVERY-WHERE. He said, "Hi, how are you?" and I said, "Hello, Justin, I'm good, how are you?" He then replied, "Good, thanks." Then the paps went mental; everyone was crowding and it was just crazy. I felt so scared, not just for myself but for Justin, it was so unsafe. He then got in the car and drove away. My friends and I headed back to the hotel. We were looking through Twitter when my friend Lauren said, "Sophia, is that you?" and it was a picture the paps took of me with Justin! Unknown to me, whilst all this was happening, my granddad was rushed into hospital – my mum never told me as it would make me want to come home, so she just left it and let me enjoy myself. I waited all night again to try to meet Justin.

'In the early hours on Wednesday morning at about 1.30am, he actually came out. We were all in complete utter shock when he walked out and said, "Hi, girls." We asked for a quick photo and he said, "Of course." We all got photos with him and spoke to him about *Believe* and the Summertime Ball. He asked if I was going and I said yes! He asked if I was excited, I said yes! In the back of my head, all I was thinking was: I can't believe this is happening. Justin then said he had to go, so I asked for a hug and he accepted. I hugged him and it felt unreal. When he was walking to his car, I shouted, "THANK YOU SO MUCH, JUSTIN!" He said, "Anytime." He is literally the most sweetest, most perfect human being you could ever meet. Trust me, he is flawless.

'I rung my mum up to tell her and I was crying my eyes out. I fell to the floor. My mum was crying too but not just because I met Justin, but because I still didn't know about my granddad. I then waited four hours for my train to come. I was absolutely exhausted and emotional; I just wanted to get home to see my granddad and my family to tell them all about my experience. When I got home, my big sister was waiting for me. I realised my granddad wasn't home, neither was my mum. My sister then told me he had been rushed into hospital. My sister gave me the option to stay home and get some sleep and go to the hospital later on, or go with her then. I chose to go with her then. I got to the hospital and saw my granddad lying there helpless, my heart was breaking; I felt it wasn't right to bring up my meeting Justin because he looked so ill.

'When he was looking a little better, I said, "Granddad, you know that boy I adore, Justin Bieber?" He slowly nodded. I then said, "Granddad, I met him!" His eyes just lit up, and he turned to me. I showed him the photo and it was the first smile we had seen from him in weeks, maybe months. He then just kept holding my hand and he said to me, "I am so happy for you," and that was the last thing he said to me. The following morning, when my mum and sister got up at 9.30am, I was supposed to be going up in the afternoon, but by 10am he passed away. So indirectly through my granddad and Justin, my dream actually came true, but not just mine, my granddad's too.

'Justin has helped me through his music to cope with the hard situation with my granddad.'

HOLLY'S STORY

Eighteen-year-old Holly is from Glasgow, Scotland. Her favourite three songs are 'Be Alright', 'Never Let You Go' and 'One Time'. Holly says: 'I love how inspirational Justin is. Despite at times the media, their rumours and negativity, he always stays humble and makes it all about the music. I also love how he always gives back, whether it's giving money to charity or visiting sick children in hospital.

'Being a Belieber in Scotland is good, but hard – hard because Justin has never toured here; he came in 2010 to perform at a secondary school and since then he hasn't been back. I've had to travel four times to see him, which makes the experience of seeing him even more exciting, but I do wish he'd come here for those who can't travel. It's good too being a Belieber here because all of the Scottish Beliebers have all come together and have worked hard to try and get Justin to come here: we're a family. I'm hopeful that Justin will tour here one day, though.

'I met Justin in London on Thursday, 13 September 2012. I've been a Belieber since 2009 and most people know me as "the girl who loves Justin Bieber". Despite Justin telling us to Never Say Never and to Believe, I always felt that my dream of meeting Justin was always going to remain a dream. I was proven wrong; I've entered so many Bieber-related competitions and I've never been lucky – at times I even wondered if there was ever any point entering them if I wasn't going to feel anything but disappointment when I didn't win. When I had found out about the Clyde 1 In: Demand Scotland Contest, I thought I would give it a try, even though I was positive I wouldn't get anywhere. I did as the competition said: I liked the picture of Justin they uploaded on their Facebook page and I waited. When the next day came I was picked as the first finalist! What?! Was this really happening to me? As the week went on, two more finalists were picked; then on the final week a 4th one was picked.

'We had to answer a question: "How many copies of Justin Bieber's album *Believe* were sold in the UK?" I had no clue whatsoever. I took a guess and guess what? I WON! I WAS MEETING JUSTIN AFTER THREE WHOLE YEARS OF WAITING! I felt so lucky, so blessed, and I was so grateful. I travelled to London on 12 September. I genuinely couldn't believe that the next day I would be meeting Justin – I didn't even know where I was meeting him, it was all kept very secret.

'On the morning of the 13th, I woke up feeling so sick with nerves, as I did every morning in the run-up to the big day! In order to pass time, my mum and I just waited outside Justin's hotel with many other Beliebers and I made so many amazing friends that I hope to stay in contact with! I met [guitarist] Dan Kanter at Pret A Manger in Oxford Street and he was so sweet; we spoke and I got a picture with him. Then we got a phone call telling us we were to go back to

Justin's hotel, where someone would come out and get us. After waiting for what seemed like forever in the cold, we got another phone call telling us to walk into the hotel, so we did. I think loads of the Beliebers were probably like, "What the hell is that girl doing?" but others were shouting, "GO, HOLLY!!" I was smiling so much.

'I was taken up to the floor Justin was staying on and, on the way up, I met [bodyguard] Kenny Hamilton and I said hi and he said hi back. Due to Justin doing his radio interviews, we had to wait a while, so as the time ticked by my nerves increased dramatically. The lift door opened and out walked Moshe (Justin's ex-bodyguard) and he went into Justin's room. When he came back, he asked if I was the competition winner and I replied yes. My mum said to him that Justin must be tired with all the interviews and the busy schedule, and Moshe smiled and said, "It's all part of the job." We were then taken to stand outside Justin's room. I could hear him talking, laughing – at one point he even sang part of "As Long As You Love Me". I was dying, I was so nervous. There is nothing better than hearing Justin singing live with only a thin wall between you and him, it was indescribable.

'Eventually the big moment came: it was my time to meet Justin; I could not believe it! I walked into his hotel room and a photographer was taking pictures of Justin. I can't even begin to explain how flawless he looked, he didn't even look real; this may seem weird but he was like a waxwork figure, he was just that perfect!! While he was getting some quick photos, Kenny shook my hand and spoke to me about Scotland. Justin began to walk over to me, smiling so big whilst looking directly into my eyes; it was unbelievable. He greeted me with "Heyyyyy, it's SO good to meet you!!" with the biggest smile and held out his arms for me to walk into for a massive hug. IT WAS THE BEST HUG EVER! It was so long, so warm and so tight; at one point during the hug he even squeezed me tighter. I didn't want to let go of him ever! I told him how I couldn't believe this was finally happening!

'We then got photos taken. he looked at me smiling and said, "I've got my One Time hoodie on today," and he seemed so happy about it because he knows how much the hoodie means to both him and us Beliebers as, for a lot of us, the "One Time" music video is what captured our hearts and made us fall in love with Justin Bieber. We had two photos taken by the photographer and I had my arms wrapped around his waist, and his hand was on my back, and then he asked if I had a camera so we could get more photos together, which I did so we got two more photos.

'He pulled me in closer to him and his face was touching mine and he was holding me; inside I was screaming. After the photos, we hugged again. When he spoke, his voice was heavenly – I never thought I'd be speaking to the boy whose voice I'm so used to hearing only on TV, on the internet, and on his albums. He asked me if I wanted him to sign anything so he signed my Bieber experience photo album. He wrote: "Holly (with a heart beside it) Believe, Justin Bieber (with a smiley face)". He made sure it was the correct spelling of my name – he was like, "Holly, it's spelt H O DOUBLE L Y, right?" – and he took his time to make it perfect! We spoke some more, I don't remember exactly what about, though 'cause I was so nervous and some of it is a blur, but basically our conversation was just like about the Believe Tour, Scottish Beliebers, etc. I gave him a letter which I had written to him, which explained how much he meant to me, how much he inspired me and how much he has helped me through difficult situations. I asked him if he could read it if he had the time, to which he replied, "Of course!"

'Justin then walked over to my mum and said, "Mom, give me a hug!" and they hugged it out. It was such a cute moment to watch because my mum knows how happy Justin makes me, and to meet him was an experience for her also. After ten-plus minutes, my time with Justin was coming to an end as he was to have something to eat and then head to the ITV Studios to film for *The Jonathan Ross Show*, so he gave me another big hug and I savoured every second of it, knowing that this was probably the only chance I'd ever get of meeting Justin Bieber. I said thank you to Justin for everything, all I could do was thank him because I'm so grateful to support someone as down-to-earth and amazing as him. We said our goodbyes and then it was over.

'When I walked out of his room, all I could do was shake and cry. What had just happened was so overwhelming and I was in so much shock. I was so grateful and it was the best ten minutes of my life! I never thought I'd have an experience like that: I personally met Justin in private, and all I can say is that he is one of the most loveliest people I have ever met, so friendly, loving, and he made me feel so comfortable, like we were best friends who hadn't seen each other for so long. I'll carry the memory of meeting Justin with me in my head and heart throughout the rest of my life! I'm so grateful to have had an opportunity like that, and I'll never take it for granted.'

CARLY'S STORY

Sixteen-year-old Carly is from Liverpool. Her favourite three songs are 'Take You', 'Overboard' and 'Never Say Never'. She says: 'There seems to be a lack of support for Justin in the UK, there are not many dedicated fans that I know personally, and people criticise him while I'm around. It hurts sometimes, but, being a Belieber, I wouldn't go back or change anything. It hurts also, knowing half the criticisms are false. People do not see the good things Justin does, only the bad, which the media exaggerates. I, along with other Beliebers, defend him as much as possible but it seems to me people in the UK are too misled by the press. Justin is supported by some or hated by others, especially after his time in the UK in March 2013.'

Carly has met Justin twice: at the O2 Arena in London and at the Telenor Arena in Oslo, Norway. When she met him in London, she admits, 'I was so mesmerised by his face I couldn't look away, it was just absolutely flawless. I whispered, "Oh my gosh! I love you so much, thank you for all you've done for me," and he replied with, "I just make music." I gave him a necklace dog-tag photo frame of him and his mother on the inside and said, "Can I give you this?" He grabbed it off me and was about to give it to his bodyguard, but looked down and saw it was of him and his mum, so put it in his pocket instead.'

Carly was interviewed by a journalist from the *Sunday People* newspaper about what it was like to meet Justin, and then she went to see the concert. She caught the T-shirt DJ Tay James threw out to the crowd and, for a few bars of 'Believe' and 'Be Alright', Justin made eye contact with her.

The second time Carly met Justin was on 16 April 2013. She had travelled all the way to Norway to see the Believe Tour concert again. She says: 'The people we were staying with had laid out four different newspapers all with Bieber headlines and left the radio on at the station where all they were talking about was Bieber Mania! Of course I couldn't understand any of it, as it was all in Norwegian but it still got me very excited!

'Getting into the outside waiting area, the atmosphere was fantastic; everywhere you looked there were Beliebers, speakers blasting Bieber music and more excited Beliebers. I waited until 4pm to check in for the Meet & Greet, just after Justin had driven past and waved to the fans in his car!

'We were then led into a line, and by this point I felt like I needed to throw up a thousand times but I was calm on the outside, and that's what mattered. Ryan [Butler] gave me the wristband and asked if my friend Benedicte was my guest – well, she was, so I said yes. He also gave Benedicte a wristband, which we weren't expecting! She was going to meet him too! A few minutes later, Nick DeMoura appeared and I had my photo taken with him, although he looked too busy to stop and chat. Dan Kanter came; he was so sweet. I hadn't seen him when I met Justin in London so I gave him a big hug and chatted to him for about five minutes before getting a photo and sitting back down. I couldn't believe it – I had actually met Dan!!!

'My seat for the concert was in Felt E, which was quite a good view. However, I was astonished to hear Ryan ask me, "Where is your seat for the concert?" I began to tell him and he cut me off with, "It doesn't matter, here's a wristband for the DIAMOND CIRCLE." I COULDN'T BELIEVE WHAT I WAS HEARING! He gave one to Benedicte too so she could come with me to the concert, even though she didn't have a ticket in the first place. I've seen Scooter [Braun] give tickets on *Never Say Never*, but I never thought that could be me!

'Excited as I was, the time came to wait in a different room and queue up for the meeting. I could feel myself collapsing on the inside, I'm shaking now just thinking about it, but I was calm on the outside, and that's what mattered. I was almost last out of the individual line, so I had time to prepare and not get myself worked up. The next words I heard were: "Step in, please, miss". Okay, Carly, be calm, prepare yourself and relax, I thought to myself. Justin was standing there, flawless in sunglasses (which I was surprised at), a hat and a black vest. I can't say I took in much information about his appearance, but, boy, I noticed his moustache! I just remember thinking he looks so hot! He was finishing up with the last people as I shyly said "Hey", walking in.

'The next few moments were the best of my life. "Can I have a hug, please?" I said, as I didn't get one last time I had seen him and I wanted to know how wonderful it felt, which it did. "Of course!" he answered. It was a little tight one, which was perfect. I had planned to say, "I'll support you through everything", and may have said that whilst hugging him, but it's a blur so I can't be sure. We then released the hug and I stood, my back to the camera (so that I could stall time a little), holding his arms. I quickly said, "Can we do a cute picture?" I could see my face in the reflection of his glasses – oh, I looked excited! Justin replied with "A cute picture? Yeah, sure."

'He slipped his hand on my waist underneath my blazer. I'm not used to people touching my stomach, so I pushed it away a little out of impulse (stupid, I know) and he withdrew it slightly, then put it straight back. I couldn't believe Justin was holding me! The picture was snapped and it was time for me to go, so sideways I held onto his arm and said, "I love you."

He responded in his raspy low voice, "I love you too." I smiled at him and walked out of the room, knowing that it went perfectly.'

Carly loved watching the concert with her dad, Benedicte and some of her friends. Even though she had seen the show before, it was still different because Justin likes to make every performance unique. Carly admits: 'He looked so good and the energy was fantastic. Even my dad says he is a Belieber now after watching the show! My favourite song was probably "Never Say Never" or "Baby", when his pants nearly fell all the way down!'

NICOLA'S STORY

Nicola is sixteen and from London. Her favourite three songs are 'Favorite Girl', 'Believe' and 'One Less Lonely Girl'. She takes part in fan events and flash mobs when she can and loves being a Belieber. Nicola says: 'It's amazing to know I'm supporting someone so humble and grateful for his fans. It's the best feeling.'

She can still remember how amazing it felt when she found out that Justin was following her on Twitter. It made all the effort she had put into sending him tweets worth it. She had wanted to meet him when he was on his My World Tour in Europe, so entered a competition on *Bieberfever.com*. Nicola explains: 'As soon as I found out about the competition, I didn't stop – I kept going, doing everything I could possibly do to meet him. Every single day, I was doing as much as I could to promote *Bieberfever.com*. I made large posters, print screens, videos on YouTube, poems and loads more. A lot of people were telling me, "You won't win, so there's no point in trying, really." I ignored them, saying, "Never say never – you'll see."

'Months passed until it was the 16th (the day before the concert). My heart was racing all day – I don't even know how I managed to get through school that day (we had a Spanish exam), my head was down the whole time because I was so nervous. I was just praying all day that I could win tickets to meet Justin Bieber. All my friends at school were wishing me luck because they knew how much it would mean to me. In class I got bored so I got out my iPod Touch, signed into my Hotmail whilst listening to "Never Say Never". On Hotmail there was nothing there. I thought to myself, okay, that's alright – I might get it later, around 6pm, if I've won the tickets.

'I kept replaying "Never Say Never", then, ten minutes later, I refreshed my Hotmail account and saw an email. My heart paused for ten seconds, so did my voice: basically, my WHOLE LIFE paused. It was an email from *Bieberfever.com* saying,

"Congratulations BieberFan". My heart was racing with excitement, I read through it several times to make sure I wasn't dreaming. I jumped out of my seat, screamed so loud the other classes had to come in and see what was going on. I shouted, "I'VE WON A MEET & GREET TO SEE JUSTIN BIEBER! MY DREAM HAS FINALLY BECOME REALITY. THEY TOLD ME IT WOULD NEVER HAPPEN, BUT IT HAS!"

'Everyone in the class was so happy for me and wished me luck – my teacher even let me go outside to ring my parents, sister and my friend to tell them that I'd won. My life couldn't get any better. After school, I came home, had dinner and did my homework. My mum and everyone was so proud of what I had done: I proved the world wrong for telling me I couldn't live my dream. I had a shower, got ready for the next day, was on Twitter for a bit, tweeting Justin about how happy I was. I was going to meet him the next day! My friends on Twitter were also very happy for me because most of them had met Justin and told me how amazing it was, and that it would be the best moment of my life, which was so true! Thursday, 17 March 2011 came: it was the day of the concert, the day I was meeting Justin Bieber!'

Nicola, her mum and her friend Lauren went to the O2 Arena for the Meet & Greet, two-and-a-half hours before the concert was due to start. She saw Kenny Hamilton twice before she walked into the room to meet Justin. Nicola says: 'I ran straight up to Justin and gave him the biggest hug ever! He was so cute, my friend was like, "Are you Justin Bieber?" He was like, "Yes, I'm Justin Bieber."

'I gave him three poems I had specially made for him to read, with my Twitter name on, telling him to direct message me whenever he can. Because in London, we say "Oi" as in like "Hey", I said it to Justin. He was like, "What does Oi mean?" Haha, that was funny! He was actually so sweet! A second later, he said, "Come on, guys, let's take a picture." I stood next to Justin whilst someone took the picture, and my friend was next to some other people we didn't know. I was so happy standing next to him. Then, towards the end, I gave him another, really big hug and I said, "I love you so much, Justin!"

'What an experience! Best, best, best, best, best moment of my life, for sure! My dreams had become reality; even though it was quite short, it was still the most amazing time of my entire life, for sure. My friend then told me Pattie was in the room, and Scooter – I didn't even realise until she told me!! From then on, my life has been the happiest. I am never going to give up on my dreams – I will always think positively, always be happy.'

VICTORIA'S STORY

Sixteen-year-old Victoria is from Littledean. Her favourite three songs are 'One Time', 'As Long As You Love Me' and 'Nothing Like Us'. Victoria first saw Justin perform during his Believe Tour, five years after becoming a Belieber. She had bought concert tickets for 4 March, but still entered a competition that O2 were running for tickets for 5 March because her dream was to go to the arena and find someone who didn't have a ticket and give them one. She worked really hard, sending lots of tweets and was delighted when she was named one of the winners.

Victoria takes up her story: 'I went with my friend on 4 March to the O2 Arena. We were really early and saw Justin's tour bus arrive. We were waiting around, it was really windy, when a really nice couple came over and gave us their Meet & Greet bracelets. They had been going to see him with their daughter but thought it would be better if real Beliebers had the opportunity. We couldn't believe it – it was all too much. Then, when I thought things couldn't get any better, an American fan came over and swapped our concert tickets for some better ones.'

Victoria spent twenty minutes chatting to Dan Kanter before meeting Justin. She says: 'Hugging Justin was amazing! Two hours earlier, I never would have thought it was possible. He had his arm around my waist and then on my shoulder – it was better than I could have ever dreamed! When I had to go, he gave me puppy eyes and looked genuinely sad. He held my hand and squeezed my fingers before I had to walk out.'

The next day, Victoria went to see the show again, this time with the tickets she had won in the competition. She explains what happened: 'I met this girl who didn't have any tickets and I asked her if she would like to go to a concert with me. She cried and I started tearing up, I was so happy!! Cody and Alli Simpson [who were supporting Justin on the tour] drove past us in their car and so did Justin's tour bus. I also met Justin's dancers – I was absolutely overwhelmed. I went to pick my tickets up and we headed off to our seats.

'We were front row on block 112, JUST WHERE THE CREW PLACE IS! I was shaking and just going mental. After Jaden [Smith], Cody [Simpson] and Carly [Rae Jepsen] performed, we had an interval and Brad walked up to us and started talking to us. We took some amazing photos with him. When Justin was performing I couldn't stop crying, I was so happy. Allison [Kaye] and Scooter [Braun] walked past us, and Scooter noticed that I was staring at him. He laughed and asked me if I was alright. I nodded and he gave me a high five.

'Twenty minutes later Ryan [Butler] was on the screen, telling people to get off their cell phones. Kenny [Hamilton] walked past us and grabbed our phones, jokingly saying, "Is that a cell phone? What are you doing with a cell phone?" It was so funny. He then gave us a big grin and walked away.

'That night when I got home, I felt like I had been dreaming for two days: I had had such an incredible time, meeting Justin, meeting his crew and meeting some amazing Beliebers!'

HARRIET'S STORY

Harriet is fourteen and from York. Her favourite three songs are 'Born To Be Somebody', 'Be Alright' and 'One Time'. She loves being a Belieber in the UK because 'Justin comes here more than some other places in Europe but it is difficult when he is here. He normally only comes to London when promoting, which is five hours away from me, but I've still managed to make the trip five times for him! Also, because he isn't here loads there is so little chance of meeting him as everyone is trying at the same time – at his hotel, radio stations, TV studios, etc. – but it's still fun and I have met some amazing people through it.

'As soon as I knew the Believe UK tickets were coming out, I went on to my Bieberfever account and got my pre-sale code! I bought tickets to see him in Sheffield, but unfortunately, around two days later, I checked my emails and saw it was cancelled. My heart sank. I thought, I bet all the tickets are sold out now, but, when I looked through my emails again, I saw that I could get some for Manchester as they had reserved some seats for Bieberfever users. I was SO happy! I then entered the Best Collection competition for Meet & Greets but unfortunately I didn't win. I lost all hope of EVER meeting Justin and I just felt empty, but I was still happy I would be seeing him on stage the next day!

'My best friend Ebonie and I arrived at the arena and we were just so hyped. Our tickets were great: Block J, Row A, seats 1 & 2. We had also made personalised tops in the hope that we would stand out and get noticed. When Justin first came on stage, Kenny [Hamilton] walked straight past me! I reached my hand out; he smiled and held it, then walked off. I was fan-girling SO MUCH!

'It was around the time when Justin was singing "Never Say Never" when I saw Allison [Kaye] walking down the aisle next to me. When she walked past, she looked at me for about five seconds, then walked off. I knew she was picking the OLLG [One Less Lonely Girl]. She walked past another two times but she didn't seem interested in me. Then "Beauty

And A Beat" was on, when I felt a tap on the shoulder. My heart froze, and I turned around. "Do you know what I'm about to ask you?" Allison said. I just froze and started hyperventilating. "Do you want to be the One Less Lonely Girl?" "YES!!!" I screamed, and turned to my best friend, who was screaming too. I held Allison's hand and started walking down the aisle, screaming at everyone I passed. I kept saying, "Thank you!!!!" to her and I just kept looking at the stage and thinking that I would be up there soon!

'When we got backstage, Allison told me what to do but I just couldn't understand anything. Everything felt like a dream, it was so magical. She said, "What's your name?" so I said, "Harriet," and she said, "What's your name tonight?" and I replied, "ONE LESS LONELY GIRL!" She was just asking me if I had my phone and making sure my shorts and top were alright, then someone was walking up to us and then I realised it was FREDO! Straight away I went and gave him a massive hug and he squeezed me! He said, "Well done!" I started crying and shaking, but Fredo told me to save it until I was out on stage and to be happy, so I did!

'Fredo gave me a high five, then started filming me. I walked up some small steps towards the stage as Fredo was still filming. Then suddenly I felt a tap on the shoulder, and it was Ryan [Butler]! I gave him a huge hug and we were just chatting – they are all SO nice, the dancers as well. I knew it was close to the part where I came onstage and I was shaking so much. I asked Allison if I could talk to Justin after, but she said he has to go straight back onstage. The dancers opened the curtains and I just focused my eyes on Justin. He turned around and reached his hand out to me. I completely forgot there were 20,000 people watching and just walked to him. He took my hand, and sat me down on the chair. His eyes were so beautiful; I was lost in them. He put the OLLG crown on me and put his hand on my back. WAS I DREAMING? JUSTIN BIEBER WAS SAT IN FRONT OF ME, SINGING TO ME! I started singing along to the words. Then he came up next to me again and put his arm on my back. I hugged him, feeling his PERFECT body. I rested my head on him – it was seriously like heaven.

'Then he came in front of me and held my hand. I was still in denial; I couldn't believe it was happening to me. When he finished the song, I gave him a hug. Justin asked, "What's your name?" "Harriet," I replied. "What?" (CAN I JUST SAY THIS WAS SO SEXY – he raised his eyebrows and he just looked beautiful.) "Harriet? Everyone, give it up for Harriet!" He stepped down, linked his arm out for me, and I stepped down and held onto his arms; I couldn't resist. I said, "I love you, Justin!" and he said, "I love you too!" and we ran off together. When we went off, Justin had to go back onstage and Allison said to me, "How was it?" and I said, "PERFECT!" We were walking back down the small stairs and I was shaking so much. I said to her, "I think I'm going to faint," and she said, "Don't do that till we are down the stairs!"

'Fredo came up to us with his camera and I said thank you to them both and we started walking back to my seat. I was so shaky, confused, happy, LOST IN CONFUSION! Just then my best friend, Ebonie, saw me and we ran to each other and gave each other the BIGGEST hug. We were both just crying with happiness!'

MARIA'S STORY

Maria is nineteen and from Clacton-on-Sea. Her favourite three songs are 'Maria' (naturally), 'Favorite Girl' and 'Take You'. She says: 'The things I love most about Justin would include his music, old and new, his caring nature and his funny personality. Being a Belieber in the UK is great as we have amazing concert venues here, where you are able to have the opportunity to see your favourite artist perform and even meet them. I have met Justin twice: the first time was in 2011, when I won a competition through his fan club, *Bieberfever.com*, and the second time was in 2013.

'It all started in 2010. I made and wore a prom dress, which is pretty much covered in pictures of Justin. The pictures I chose showed Justin growing up and the journey he had been on with his team. I'm nineteen now, so, when I think back, I honestly do not know how I came up with such a crazy idea. I uploaded a picture of me wearing my prom dress on Twitter. The response was mixed – some people thought I had lost my mind but most Beliebers loved the dress. Today the Twitpic has over 11,000 views. Including Justin, hell yeahhh! That night he direct messaged me on Twitter, saying: 'Have an amazing prom…that dress. wow. dont know what to say. thank u.' I was so shocked and happy that he had finally [seen] all the hard work and support that I had put into the dress.

'Then I heard about Justin's official fan club, Bieberfever, and decided to sign up. It was around the time that he announced his My World Tour dates and Bieberfever had a contest to win a Meet & Greet. I remember the day before the concert when I found out that I had won: my family was screaming the house down! I wore my prom dress to the concert so I could show Justin. I took my sister along to the Meet & Greet with me. We walked in, and our picture was taken straight away. I walked round in front of Justin and said, "Do you like my dress?" He paused and replied, "Yes, it's amazing – I remember you off Twitter!"

'When Justin announced the Believe Tour, I entered the contest on Bieberfever. Reliving memories, I won a Meet & Greet. I took my dress with me into the Meet & Greet and left the corner hanging out of my bag. I walked in first and talked to Justin about my dress. He grabbed the corner and he was asking me all about it, looking confused. I asked if he remembered me. "I always remember you guys," he said. Then he pulled me to the side to take the picture. I love how my hair is over Justin's shoulder in the photo: it's cute! I put my arms out to give him a hug, and he smiled and put his arms out for a hug too. As we were walking out, my sister shook his hand. I looked back at Justin and he winked at us!! I melted.'

PIPPA'S STORY

Sixteen-year-old Pippa is from Staffordshire. If she had to name her favourite three songs she would pick one from *My World*, one from *My World 2.0* and another from *Believe*. She explains: 'It tends to change, but I'd choose "Down To Earth" from *My World* as my favourite song. When I first heard this song, back in

January 2010, I instantly fell in love with it – I can relate to it a lot. My second favourite would be "Up" from *My World 2.0*, it's a really beautiful song. My third favourite would have to be "Catching Feelings", but I love so many songs from Justin's *Believe* album, it's really hard to choose a favourite.

'I am a Belieber because I love how Justin interacts with his fans: he always shows that he appreciates all their support and love. I admire all the charity work he does – it doesn't get shown much in the media spotlight, they only tend to post the negative about him, but he does so much good. It was announced recently that he is the biggest Make-A-Wish giver in music history – a huge achievement. It's great to be a UK Belieber, we always come together to help one another. We also work hard on promoting Justin – for example, when "Boyfriend" got released, the UK was the only country in the world not to have it on iTunes as the label made it go on radio first. We all came together and requested it like mad, and it ended up being the most requested song on BBC Radio 1 and Capital FM. After the hard work we put in, we managed to get the "Boyfriend" release date moved forward. Another time we worked together to promote Justin was when "Believe" was released. The experts thought that Justin wouldn't get to No. 1 over here, but we all worked hard promoting and he proved them wrong and got to No. 1.'

Pippa has met Justin twice: at a top-secret book signing for *Just Getting Started* and before his concert in Birmingham. She reveals: 'I was on my way to the train station, tweeting on my phone, when all of a sudden I got a mention saying, "Congrats on the RT!" so I went onto Justin's Twitter page and saw that he RT'd me, so then I start freaking out! After the train journey, I finally arrived in London and went straight to the "secret location" where the book signing was being held. Once I got to the venue I saw at least 200 people queuing up already. I joined the queue. The line started to move slowly and after around an hour of waiting, I finally got inside and got given a copy of *Just Getting Started*. I walked into the hall and saw a stage with a black curtain drawn and loads of Beliebers sitting on the floor, reading through the book. Whilst waiting in line for Justin to come, I was on my phone on Twitter and all of a sudden I see that Justin has RT'd me again – like seriously? I was in line waiting to meet him and he RT'd me twice in the space of a couple of hours. Could my day get any better?

'Fast forward to two hours later, all of a sudden everyone starts screaming and I see this pink/red sleeve behind the curtain: Justin. Everyone starts screaming "Justin" and then he started teasing us all by popping his head out of the curtain. He then ran across stage and waved to everyone. After about thirty minutes, the line started to move really quick and, before I knew it, it was my turn to meet him. I walked in and saw him sitting at a table. I gave him my book to sign, which he did and then he looked up, smiled and said, "Here you go."

'The second time I met Justin was at one of his Birmingham shows on the Believe Tour. I was lucky enough to have a Meet & Greet after saving up for over a year to be able to buy one. I met him with my friend from Twitter, Nafisa. It was worth every penny: Justin gave me a side hug and rubbed my back, it was magical! I really hope I get to meet him again one day soon.'

TARA'S STORY

Tara is seventeen and from London. Her favourite three songs are 'Believe', 'One Less Lonely Girl' and 'Love Me Like You Do'. She says: 'I love the relationship Justin has with his Beliebers, like the way he always tweets about how special we are to him. He also really inspires me. I think it's amazing how much he has achieved – he was just a kid from a small town in Canada and now he is a worldwide star. He helps me to believe that anything is possible if you work hard enough for it.

'There are a lot of Beliebers in the UK so that's nice and you can buy merchandise literally everywhere. I also like the way we speak the same language as Justin here because I would get so confused if we didn't.

'In April 2012, I first properly tried to meet Justin in London. I found out he was actually quite near where I live so I went with my friend from school. When we got there, we made friends with about seven other Beliebers and we decided to stand by a door where nobody else was standing, as the other entrance was crowded with people trying to meet him. We had been there ages and nothing was happening so I went to talk to some other people I knew, who were standing literally a few metres up the road. As I turned and started walking, Justin came to that door where we were standing. I didn't know as none of them told me. He let them all in. They all met Justin as I was walking away. When my friend came out screaming, telling me what had just happened, I was so upset – I thought I was never going to meet him. After that I tried to meet him every day he was in London and failed.

'A few months later, he came back, but I still didn't get to meet him and I really started to lose hope. Then, on 21 February 2013, my dream finally came true. I went with my friend Bailey, who also had back luck with him in the past. When we found out he was back in London, we knew we had to go. We found out the hotel and got there at around 8am. We were the first ones there but, as time went on, more people started showing up. At about 10am, all of Justin's crew started getting on the tour bus. We were so excited as this meant he was coming out soon. I was looking towards the door when I saw somebody wearing a snapback and multicoloured high-tops walking out the door. It was Justin! I couldn't believe it was finally happening. Everyone was screaming and shouting. I just stayed quiet, hoping he would come over. He started walking towards me and took my phone to take a picture. I just remember seeing us together on the screen and I just couldn't believe it. He took the picture, said, "Thank You," and gave me my phone back; I was in shock. It was quick, but I don't care – I had just met Justin Bieber! It didn't hit me until I told my mum on the phone and I just started crying: it had finally happened.

'The next day, just when I thought it couldn't get any better, my friend texted me saying she had a spare ticket to his book signing and I could have it. I couldn't believe how much my luck was changing! When we got there, there must have been hundreds of Beliebers queuing up. It took a while as we were quite near the back, but we finally got close. When it was my turn I told him how amazing he is and he looked up at me and said, "No, you are," and signed my book. Security was pushing me away so that's all I really got, but I don't mind – at least I got to talk to him, even if it was for only two seconds. I am so grateful for everything that happened and I still can't believe it!'

AMY'S STORY

Sixteen-year-old Amy lives in Uxbridge, West London. She says: 'If I had to pick my top three songs I'd say "One Time" (because it's a classic and that was the first song he ever released. It reminds me how it all started), "Fall" (I just think this is a beautiful song and it has so much meaning behind the lyrics) and "Believe" (this song is the title song of Justin's album and it's just so heart-warming to see how far he's come and how much he's grown into a great musician).

'The thing I love the most about Justin is that he never fails to put his fans first. He's not like any other celebrity – he treats his fans like family and never fails to thank us for the support we give him or just ask how our day is going.

'Personally, I think I'm extremely lucky to live in London because, apart from touring, Justin only comes to London when he visits England. I love making friends with all the other Beliebers in

London and, although Justin doesn't come here all the time, it's always so much fun when he does. In April 2011, I organised a Bieber Parade in London with my two friends. It was a great success, with over 60 Beliebers attending. We raised over £200 for Pencils of Promise. In July 2011, I attended the pre-release of *Never Say Never* in HMV Oxford Street. Around 200 Beliebers were let into the store and the doors were closed. We all sang Bieber Karaoke, got merchandise and even received a private message from Justin. In October 2011, we held another Bieber Parade to promote Justin's new album at the time, *Under The Mistletoe* – this was also a great success. I also attended a buy-out for this album, where we all brought the CD and they were then donated to the teens on the ward at the Teenage Cancer Trust Unit. In March 2012, I attended a Parade to celebrate Justin's 18th birthday. This was so much fun and we raised a lot of money. Not many events have taken place since as Justin began touring; however, I'm attending a few more events this year for Justin's perfume, new music and to raise money for charity.'

> **DID YOU KNOW?**
>
> Three million copies of Justin's *Under The Mistletoe* album were sold worldwide, making it one of the biggest albums of 2011.

Amy has been a Belieber since 2009 and has been fortunate enough to meet Justin four times. The first time she met him was at the Royal Garden Hotel in Kensington on 25 April 2012. She had been waiting outside the hotel with twenty other girls when Justin came out and got in a car. Amy explains: 'All the girls ran into the road but me and my friend stood on the pavement. Justin rolled down the window and said, "Hey, girls!" I replied with, "Thank you for being my inspiration, Justin – I love you." He then said, "Never give up on your dreams, ever. You need to believe," and the car pulled away with Justin waving at us.

'The next time I met Justin was on 6 June 2012. It was the two-year anniversary of me first ever seeing Justin. I got up at 4am and waited outside The Langham hotel from 5am with my best friend. We had to wait a long time but, at 2pm, Justin came outside. He walked straight over to me (you can see this on the "All Around The World" video, three minutes, eight seconds in). He hugged me and asked how I was doing. I then got pictures with Justin and he signed my NY Yankees purple cap. I then gave him a bracelet with Union Jack beads on and said, "This is from your UK Beliebers – you might not always be here but, wherever you are, we'll always support you." He hugged me and replied with, "Thank you, sweetie." He then got pictures with my friends before heading off to Radio 1.

'The third and fourth times that I met Justin were at signings. The third time was pretty quick and Justin said, "Hey!" as soon as I walked in. I asked how his day was and thanked him before he signed my book; this was on 12 September 2012. The fourth time that I met Justin was on 23 February 2013. We (me and four of my friends) were some of the first in the queue to meet Justin. The five of us walked into the room and they shut the door behind us. I just looked at Justin, gob-smacked at how amazing he looked. I turned to my friend and said, "We should sing, when will we ever be able to do this again?" I sing a lot and I've been so inspired by Justin (my YouTube is amykathrynwebber and my Bieber YouTube is bieberlovass).

'So we began singing the chorus of "Beauty And A Beat". Justin looked up immediately and a smile spread across his face and he began to sing along. By the time I got to the table, my friends had been escorted out of the room. "Thank you, Kidrauhl, you honestly don't know how happy you make all of us and I don't know what I'd do without you, I love you," I said. As soon as I called him by his nickname Kidrauhl, he looked at me and grabbed my hand. "Thank you, I'll always be here for you too. Love you lots," he replied, as he handed me my book.

'I'm extremely lucky to have met and seen Justin a lot of times and I don't take it for granted for a second. Being a Belieber has helped me to meet what I'd call some of my best friends. I enjoy every second of supporting Justin and we've come so far. The future is looking bright and I can't wait to see what opportunities lay around the corner.'